The Art of Chain

by

Fischer Garrett and Cecilia T. Winters

The Art of Chain
A Guide to Steel Restraint

All text and chain bondage work by Fischer Garrett and Cecilia T. Winters
Interior and book cover mosaic photography by Cecilia T. Winters
Book cover design by Fischer Garrett
www.TheArtOfChain.com
Book cover background photography (artistic chain w/ lighting) by Mistress Sara

ISBN: 978-1-942733-00-3
EPub: 978-1-942733-01-0
Mobi: 978-1-942733-02-7
PDF: 978-1-942733-03-4

NOTICE

Personal responsibility is a basic tenet of adult activity. Like any adult activity, chain bondage inherently contains risk of both physical and emotional injury. Any information or safety guidelines provided in this book are solely suggestions on ways to help reduce those inherent risks. By deciding to engage in any adult activity, including those detailed in this book, you are taking on physical and emotional responsibility for your own actions, and agree to hold harmless all individuals associated with the creation, publication, and sale of this book.

Table of Contents

Introduction

Bondage. The word means something both specific and varied to so many different people. To the Top it means to restrain decoratively, functionally, or both. To the Bottom it can mean to be placed in captivity: to be captured and or restrained in positions that put them at a consensual loss of physical autonomy. Bondage is simultaneously an act, a state of mind and body, a thing to exist in, and an implication of control.

The subject here is the "B" of the core tenants of BDSM (*Bondage, Dominance/Discipline, Submission/ Sadism, Mastery/Masochism*). For this book, the other three are mostly irrelevant except in the context of an implicit power dynamic that exists between the bondage Top and the bondage Bottom. There is an agreed upon social convention that one places and the other receives. Surely a wide debate exists about what the acronym actually stands for, but it is not important here. For that there are other references to seek out, which is left as an exercise to you, the reader.

This book starts at a point in our journey around 2018, when we started practicing this form of bondage with chains, and culminates in a three year development of everything we have created to teach the basics of this material to date. There are other topics, such as suspension, which we have deemed too advanced than what should be taught at the starting point of chain bondage. Learning and practicing suspension bondage poses a more significant set of physical and mental health risks that are probably unwise to jump into if this is the first time you're reading about bondage. Obviously, we can't tell you what you should and shouldn't do, as you will notice our usage of disclaimers throughout, but you should at least have an idea that using bondage techniques to hold a person fully or partially up off of the ground is not a trivial feat.

The techniques we have developed rely on applications of engineering and industrial devices, which is not to say that they are foolproof. Many of the items we have acquired for use usually have a strict-sounding disclaimer that goes something like this: "NOT FOR USE ON HUMANS", which we obviously have discarded, thus voiding the warranty of all these devices.

We have done our best to give what we perceive to be a good course of guidance on how to use them to restrain a human, regardless of race, color, sex, gender, shape, and ability. It is your job as a bondage Top to put them to use to your most comfortable level of shared risk, wherever that may fall.

If your level of risk includes using chain bondage to put someone in interesting and fun positions for aesthetics, art, pleasure, pain, or sex, then keep reading!

Chapter 1 - The Why

If the introduction piqued your curiosity sufficiently, then welcome! This is the first step in your chain bondage path.

We enjoy chain bondage as a functional and aesthetic art form. It has a really great classic kink look and harkens back to one of the things kink is known for aside from the whips, crops, handcuffs, and other generic staple icons of the Lifestyle.

Visual Aesthetic

Chain does a great job of capturing and reflecting light. The surface finish provides an excellent opportunity for incident light sources to highlight the path that chain takes around a body, showing off angles, curves, and bondage intensity. It offers hundreds, if not thousands, of tiny mirrors that sparkle and shine like jewelry for the body. It has an appearance that screams "I am restrained and I cannot move."

Chain implies heft; a strength of material that cannot easily be broken or escaped from. The visual arts have demonstrated chain as an icon of immobility. In modern times chains are used to keep large items enclosed in a secure, mechanical industrial fashion. In kink it tells the story that "I am trapped here, on the wall and cannot escape."

Functionality

Chain is incredibly modular. When you browse a hardware store and while in the chain aisle, one of the things you might notice is the wide diversity of connecting devices in all different sizes, shapes, finishes, and strengths. The great thing is that as long as you match up the right size and strength of connector with the size and strength of the chain you're pretty much set to get started! There is very little learning curve required to put a connector anywhere on the chain itself. It works as it looks. There is no other manipulation of the chain required.

Ease of Placement

Chain goes on a human very easily, which we will demonstrate in this book. The fundamental placement patterns that you will learn have some flexibility according to preference and comfort/discomfort of the Bottom. Though application of tension will be critical to sustaining chain bondage on a body, it is unsophisticated and you may find that you can apply the techniques shown very quickly. Once you have a good grasp on how the connectors are secured on the chain and how your hands must move in order to make that happen (through practice as muscle memory is imperative) the modification of any of the techniques shown will become easier over time.

Fetishism

Chain and chain connectors are industrial. They are utilitarian. They represent a kind of warehouse, rigging style of bondage that isn't found anywhere else. Chain falls into the traditional ideas of *hardcore bondage*. It is even mentioned in a pop song that "...chains and whips excite me", a ballad written about S & M.

If you go to any dungeon or private play room, you'll see the presence of chains somewhere, whether it be hanging from a ceiling, attached to a wall, or dangling from a St. Andrew's Cross. Chains are a ubiquitous element of the kink scene.

Goals

Let's face it: you're likely reading this because the idea of restraining someone in steel hardware stirs up something inside you, whether it is artistic, sensual, erotic, sexual, or of any other nature. You want to engage in sharing a bondage experience with another person for some kind of objective, whatever that is.

When we first started doing chain bondage, Fischer had the exact same feeling. He wanted to be able to perform a bondage technique that was more easily understood and less overwhelming than other bondage techniques, with about the same cost and barrier to entry, and that allowed him to accomplish the kinds of artistic/graphic/aesthetic objectives they wanted to meet. For the most part, they've been able to make this come true.

It is a fact that other bondage methods exist, but while they look awesome, it just never *clicked* in a way that chain bondage did, and with a little creativity and understanding of the approaches outlined in this book, almost anyone can accomplish some of those goals as well.

Considerations

As with the first law of thermodynamics A.K.A. conservation of energy, "There is no such thing as a free lunch." Everything has a cost, and they are outlined here. These are important to appreciate in order to reap the full knowledge of applying chain bondage onto a Bottom.

The first is that it is good to think of the quantity of chain and connectors utilized as a "material budget." This budget dictates what you can and cannot do in chain bondage. It consists of how many...

- ...connectors of a type that you have
- ...different types of connectors that you have
- ...chain link segments you have in total
- ...chain link segments of a specific length you have

This may seem complicated at first, but this pattern of thinking will make sense as you progress throughout this book. Starting off with a small amount of chain and connectors will help you familiarize yourself with keeping track of these *automagically*. Part of the goal of chain bondage is to develop and apply the most effective restraint you can with the least expensive cost, or using your budget efficiently.

Another important aspect of chain bondage is to develop the skill to estimate sizing someone up for the amount of chain and connectors in your budget. This will make perfect sense if you have ever used a fabric measuring tape or know by number any of you or your Bottom's clothing sizes.

Conversely, this is possible to do if you have an idea of how to shop for clothing when specific sizes are listed on the tag of the apparel.

If you have never measured yourself, or a Bottom, now is an excellent opportunity to get more acquainted with determining bodily proportions in a more intimate and personal way than you ever have been before. Besides, if it gives you the opportunity to purchase or make correctly fitted clothing for someone as a gift as a result, you've just given yourself some solid bonus points. Congratulations!

The last thing to consider is that this will help you develop a sense of where, how, and the order in which all things go together. This is a similar skill to assembling toy building blocks, or putting together contemporary Swedish furniture, but far less involved. When we first developed a lot of these techniques, it was not always obvious, especially when putting the bondage on and taking the bondage off. Removal of the bondage is not always reversing the steps!

Once you learn the basics of assembly, the process will make much more sense and you'll be on your way to mastering the art.

What is Covered

This book is intended to cover what we think are the complete fundamentals of chain bondage techniques which includes ways and places to attach chain and connectors/devices; "columns", which are ways to place bondage around a body segment; harnesses, or predetermined patterns for placing chain on a body that serve a specific purpose; some static poses that can be used for art, photography, decoration, and sex, and finally 'decorative' bondage that isn't necessarily functional as a harness but works as both a restraint and *a look*.

While you may not necessarily feel that you need to know all of the technical details explained in Chapters One through Four *there are important safety details about the hardware used in this form of chain bondage that should not be neglected.* Some of the details about the types of chain available will directly relate to the kind of hardware that can be used and how it can be applied. The details on chain maintenance are also important because chains that degrade through applications other than "regular use" have a real environmental and financial hit. Everything we have chosen to put in this book has been included for a reason.

As with any other new skill there are nuances that are hard to learn. Some of these have to do with proper tensioning. Some of them involve placement and manipulation of connecting devices. Others like hand positioning, dexterity, and object orientation are relative to the bondage Top and are not always intuitive. We hope to do our best to illustrate ways to do multiple things at the same time with the equipment that is involved. This will make more sense in photos when we demonstrate chain and connector placement and illustrate some of the minor physical complexities.

In addition to the pure bondage techniques, we're also going to explain safety, our position on consent, negotiation, risks, and our philosophy of equality and inclusiveness. These are tenants of kink that we hold dear and believe that they have a significant importance to creating not only a healthy bondage relationship with yourself and others, but a better alternative lifestyle scene as well.

It should be noted that some of the bondage displayed shows chain placed directly on human skin or clothing that can support bondage. In this context it is purely from a functional perspective (but reaching a wider audience with tamer imagery might not be such a bad thing, either). A bottom does not have to be naked to participate in chain bondage and you should not accept that as the *de facto* position to negotiate from.

While this is not a book on performing self bondage, much of the content could be done on yourself with the exception of Arms-Front and Arms-Behind Chest Harnesses shown in Chapter Four. The approach to building harnesses and columns may be different than what is outlined but don't let that discourage you from trying.

Chapter 2 - Negotiation, Consent, and Risks

Negotiation and consent are some of the cornerstones of bondage scenes (sessions), kink relationships, and healthy alternative lifestyle communities. Without them, or with poor negotiations and consent practices, there are opportunities--intentional and unintentional--to commit great harm upon a Bottom and even on a Top.

Negotiation is the practice of discussing physical, mental, and emotional limits and interests with the person you intend to have a bondage scene with and coming to a mutual agreement about them. A negotiation can even occur with just yourself!

Think of a negotiation as a social contract between players. The both of you put on the table your interests in bondage, which can be such things as intensity, duration, methods, positions, or any other goals you would like to achieve. You then both come to an agreement on a mutual understanding of expectations for the scene. There should be a consensus <u>before</u> the scene takes place.

If the negotiation has been finalized consent between the players is typically established. It is now the responsibility for you both to uphold the consent agreement for the scene that is to take place.

It is important to note that negotiation and consent should occur when all participants can give sober, informed, and enthusiastic or affirmative responses. Failure to be able to give a sober, informed, and enthusiastic or affirmative response should be an indication that the negotiation has broken down somewhere and consent has not been given. Consent can be revoked at any time, even retroactively, if one or more parties have determined that consent was obtained through coercion or by other manipulative means.

<u>Lack of consent or response does not imply consent</u>. It is well established within the modern cultural landscape of alternative lifestyles that activity performed without clear, informed, sober consent is considered a violation of that consent. Societally and socially this is generally accepted as a truth.

Your bodily autonomy matters during a scene. As a Top, it is your responsibility to accept the choices made by a Bottom on where they prefer to have or to not have bondage on their body. You can decline to perform requested bondage that is outside of your risk profile or your capability.

As a Bottom, you are well within your right to determine where you would like to experience bondage. You can also say no to something proposed to you that you think is more than what you are capable of. A Top who pressures you to do something you don't want to should be someone to be wary of. Make sure your negotiations specifically include boundaries and limits about touching in places that are sexual and non-sexual for you. There is no excuse for non-negotiated sexual interaction in a scene.

A very important discussion of touch involves the potential for bondage to cause feelings of gender, body, and identity affirmation or dysphoria. It is necessary to communicate in your negotiation the possibility for feelings that might occur surrounding either of these outcomes especially if they are unwanted or undesirable. If you know that bondage placed on your body in some places or fashions causes you to have a response and it hasn't been considered by the Top in the negotiation, be sure to assert the importance of it to you. Conversely it might be good form as a Top to ask if someone might have those responses as a part of your negotiation as a regular practice. There is no way to correctly assume that someone will or will not have those responses but missing the opportunity to treat a Bottom with dignity and respect in regards to these issues during a bondage scene is an overlooked injustice.

The concept of a power dynamic can be a part of a negotiation, but there are many more books written about this subject that cover it in greater detail than we will here.

How you negotiate and establish what you consent to has a lot to do with what your risk profile is, meaning what you decide to allow to happen to you along with all of the potential negative and positive repercussions that can occur.

A big part of bondage (and BDSM or 'kink' in general) is the idea of ending a scene with a "safeword". These can be silly or serious things said or communicated that should indicate that the scene needs to stop which should also be a part of the negotiation. The fallibility of the safeword breaks down when someone in the scene refuses to consent to the operation of the safeword being communicated.

It is important to establish a way for a bondage scene to end, but it is not the fault of the Bottom if the safeword does not end up being the "magic bullet" for the scene to stop. Just as the Bottom's safeword to end the scene should be respected, the Top should also have a way to end the scene if necessary. "Common" safewords are 'RED', 'STOP', or silly words like 'Banana'. It is up to the judgment of the participants to determine if they perceive the others will respect the safeword execution but the fault for not respecting the safeword is assigned to the one who did not.

It should be noted that despite this sounding very official and formal negotiation and consent doesn't have to happen this way. It can look like a conversation; a series of text, private, or email messages; a formalized checklist and agreement document; an interview; or a handwritten letter. It should look like something that makes you feel comfortable in an open and honest conversation without deceit, extortion, or other manipulation. If anything feels wrong then trust your instinct.

As it Relates to Chain Bondage

There are quite a few aspects to negotiation as it relates specifically to Chain Bondage. This is not an all-encompassing list and there may be some that you think about that are not listed here. They are equally as important and should be included in your negotiations and risk profiles.

The first is to consider the physical sensitivities of your body. Do you have problems coming into contact with possible extreme temperatures? Steel chain is a fair conductor of heat and acquiesces to temperatures well, whether it is cold or it is hot. In the place where your bondage scene will occur is the air conditioning running on high? Is there a lack of air conditioning? Most assuredly you will feel it on your body initially, but eventually there will be a thermal equilibrium and it will match your own external body temperature. Is it humid in your environment? Damp air can make the chain harder to manipulate and you may need something to keep your hands dry during placement.

As the chain primarily shown in this guide is made from Zinc-plated Steel, it can be affected by temperature greatly. If the chain was extra chilly, how would that affect the Bottom in the scene?

It's very likely that they might react in an unpleasant way. Some people dislike the cold very much and it should be something to be aware of when you're practicing chain bondage in some environments.

Another question to ask yourself is do you have sensitivities to sound? The sound of steel chains against themselves, or landing on a floor can be a distraction. Do you have prior traumas that are associated with the sounds of chains that might trigger a panic or anxiety attack? Does the sound trigger any PTSD for you? These issues could be reduced by the Top being more cautious and considerate about the handling of the chain bondage during the scene.

The third is to reveal if you have any allergies to metal. Steel, Stainless Steel, and Zinc as well as other trace metals are something you will very likely come into contact with in a chain bondage scene.

It is entirely possible that you will not know if you have an allergy until it occurs. Do you have a plan in place if such a reaction happens? Direct contact with the skin can be mitigated by having the bondage placed over high-friction clothing such as cotton, or some types of denim. Spandex, neoprene, polyester, and other "stretchy" blends are not necessarily a good choice on account of allowing the chain bondage to slide around the body in unwanted ways.

The next critical topic to discuss is any current or prior injuries or medical restrictions that might limit or prohibit you from participating in bondage. If you have a serious injury or health problem it will limit the kinds of positions and predicaments that you could be in. Are you on any medications such as blood thinners, anti-motion sickness prescriptions, muscle relaxants, painkillers, blood pressure medication, or any medications that may have adverse or serious side effects? That may mean that chains on certain parts of your body under certain tension might not be a wise choice. It could mean that you have a higher risk of passing out under the right circumstances. Are you diabetic? This could be critical because the messages your body conveys while under stress in bondage may not be present or they might be different. Indicators like limb feeling or temperature may not be reliable enough to know if there could be an impending problem.

Do you have mobility or postural restrictions? Do you have any issues related to sitting or standing for long periods of time? These can play a factor in the situations you can be in, or put someone in. It might mean having to be more creative in your approach to bottoming or topping.

Do you have health insurance? What should happen to you if you become injured? Can you afford to go to the emergency room? These answers vary from person to person, and from locality to locality. Insurance and emergency room costs can be different from state to state in the US, and those costs can be radically different in other countries as well. Having a plan in the event of a major injury, even if the injury is not immediately apparent, is something that any participant should consider. This also goes for mental health triggers, too. What should happen if you have a trigger or a panic attack? What kind of care do you need if something happens? What will recovery from an incident look like for you?

Food and water play critical parts of determining what kind of scene you are able to do. If you haven't eaten or had enough water to drink it might be that your session is considerably shorter and less intense. Some people experience physiological effects during and after bondage and low blood sugar may be something to be concerned about.

If any of these concerns applied to you, **it does not mean you cannot participate in chain bondage.** It only means that you should take them into account in determining your level of participation whether you are a Top or a Bottom.

Specific Risks in Chain Bondage

Unlike other alternative lifestyle activities there are a set of specific types of incidents that can happen during a chain bondage scene that you might want to consider as a part of developing your risk profile.

Some of the obvious ones are the possibility of having bruises, marks, or other skin injuries happen. As scenes go on longer and longer, sweat can cause the chain to stick to the skin causing chafing or in more extreme cases pulled or stretched skin.

Injuries that are even less obvious but still likely with somewhat decreasing severity include cuts and metal splinters from surface and machining imperfections in the chain and connectors. Not all chain is made equally. Some chain links will have more burrs than others. Some brands and types of chain will have better surface finishes than others. Some connectors have design hazards that are more likely to cause an issue for the Top than the Bottom and will need to be avoided. These can generally be mitigated entirely or reduced by paying a lot of attention during routine inspections of the chain and the use of a small file to remove metallic imperfections, and understanding the risks of how some connectors operate.

Less obvious but more significant can be nerve impingement or damage. It is very possible that some parts of the bondage can press or pull on areas where a main nerve is located. There are considerable issues involved in the intensity of damage and the recovery can be difficult and long if less attention and care is used when applying the bondage. These risks can generally be mitigated by knowing and understanding what these sensations tend to feel like and what some rudimentary signs of nerve damage are. There are bondage books and online materials written that cover this topic in great length and for the sake of avoiding redundancy and being better informed we highly suggest you seek them out.

Nerves can be an issue as bondage may affect areas where sensitivity is different due to residual surgical scarring. Some people have had surgery in which scars can be quite significant and they may not know when there is a suffered injury should anything occur on those locations. It could be true as well that they cannot endure any bondage on a location where those scars exist, either physically or psychologically. In some cases bondage may cause triggers to occur. Including these in your negotiations will go some way to preventing a potential misstep in a scene.

More obvious and more significant are issues such as broken bones or joint dislocation. They are absolutely possible and should be considered before and during the engagement of a scene. What will be your plan if this happens? This would be a good time to revisit the medical paragraph in the previous section.

Falling can be a very obvious and very significant risk especially if the Bottom is in bondage that restricts movement that is instinctual in preventing fall damage. In the event of a forward fall, not having the ability to move the arms out or being able to turn to avoid a gnarly incident could be a very serious problem in a very short amount of time.

Significant ways to reduce the chances of incidents happening are things like never leaving your Bottom unattended, or not putting them in a position where falling is a higher risk. The risks are never zero.

Falls can account for a wide variety of serious injuries especially to the head, neck, shoulders, face, spine, ankle, knee, wrist, elbow or any other area that tends to be centered around a major joint. Less obvious but longer lasting results of a fall can be traumatic brain injuries (TBI); a common one being a concussion. Significant research has come out about the seriousness and longevity of these injuries that should not be overlooked.

Very unlikely but also something to think about is the risk of death during a scene. It is terrible to consider that someone could meet their end as a result of bondage but it has been known to happen even if the likelihood is very, very small.

Mental health issues can absolutely be a risk and they should not be understated. Everyone has different life experiences and it's important to think about how to help someone during a potential trigger from bondage. The things that can cause triggers is a crucial conversation that should take place before any type of bondage scene occurs (see previous sections on negotiation and risks).

It may seem as if most of these risks are Bottom-centric but in fact many of them are Top-centric risks as well. Cuts and injuries from poor surface finishes and connectors can happen to the hands. Bruises, abrasions and pinches can happen due to poor connector and chain handling. Depending on how you are able to handle holding different parts of the chain together, minor dislocations in the hand and fingers can be a risk. Experiencing emotional distress from an attempt to get a Bottom out of a precarious position can be very intense. Dropping chains or connectors on your foot can be unpleasant as well.

While this is not an exhaustive list, anything that comes up that might be important to you as a Top or a Bottom matters, and should be discussed as a part of the negotiation.

Chapter 3 - Hardware and Safety

But first, a disclaimer:

Anything that is shown in this book is only to be performed at <u>YOUR OWN RISK.</u> Bondage can be a dangerous activity and the techniques shown going forward are performed under the assumption that you are choosing to participate in this activity under your own cognizance and consent. You assume responsibility for anything that causes harm to yourself, another person, property, being, creature, or any other thing that exists that hasn't been mentioned. These techniques have not been vetted by any agency, manufacturer, body, association, or individual as being safe.

The authors and participants in the photos of this book are aware of the risks and have adjusted their risk profiles accordingly.

Chain Materials

Chain comes in a lot of different finishes, sizes, and shapes. Not all chain is created equally with the same capabilities. Some chain is *thicc*, some is small. Some chain is twisty and some is not. Some chain is shiny and some is painted or coated with a specialized treatment against environmental exposure. Some is decorative and some is functional.

This wide variety can create some confusion about what constitutes a "good" chain to use for bondage. A cursory search across different social media platforms for 'chain bondage' or 'chainbondage' reveals different ideas about what it is and what is suitable for different considerations of bondage, although that is an entirely different digression.

The choices we have made for this style of chain bondage are very explicit despite the many types available in the market today. There are pros and cons to each choice and they are listed from "most expensive" to "least expensive," as there is an up-front cost to any kind of kinky activity. The cost also depends on your level of curiosity and involvement but this book should help you consider where to start.

Chain is sold per foot or per container (box, drum, etc.) If you buy in bulk, you will need to acquire a method to cut it if you do not already have one. Technically bolt cutters will do, but they require the most amount of effort to operate. Cutting power tools are far more efficient but they come with a caveat that you will need to acquire cutting wheels at a steady pace.

Typical metal cutting wheels are made of a compacted abrasive material that wears down with every cut. There are machines that are hand operated that cut chain links with compression. These are often used in hardware stores, but probably are not practical for the home unless by reading this book you have elected to become a chain supplier and wholesaler. In which case, I might want to hear from you.

Stainless Steel

Stainless Steel chain is by far the most expensive and most attractive looking chain of the finishes. Typically sold as "316 SS" or "304 SS", it offers the greatest protection against oxidizing agents and can be sterilized more readily without harm to the finish than other types. The finish on stainless steel chain is usually much more consistent as a result of the way it is made. Stainless is also not harmful to human contact. There's an implicit advantage to using stainless steel chain in that many of the connectors used in the techniques shown are also made of similar grades of stainless which helps avoid corrosion issues in atypical environmental conditions.

The disadvantage of stainless is that the cost can be at least two to three times the cost of "regular" style chain that is employed here. We do not recommend for beginners to acquire stainless chain at the beginning due to the larger initial cost.

Stainless can be cleaned with mild detergents and drying thoroughly afterwards.

"Regular", or Zinc plated

Zinc-plated chain is a great basic material to start doing bondage with. The zinc plated finish is non-toxic, and has a slightly 'flashier' appearance. Because the chain is plated, the finish can be irregular and could need deburring. Stress over time on the chain can cause the finish to chip away, but it is not very common for this to happen. Chips usually represent themselves as **burrs** which should be removed during regular inspection and maintenance with a small file. It can also be cleaned with mild detergent, but it needs to be rinsed and dried fully afterwards to avoid corrosion.

Zinc plated chain is also not as heavy as stainless, and typically offers the same level of material strength.

A two-foot section of Zinc-plated chain.

A disadvantage of zinc-plated chain is that not all of it in the market is created equally. Some manufacturer specifications have slightly different subtle textural aspects than others, and it is up to preference which brand is preferred. It may be the case that production is irregular within batches as well causing one section to require more inspection and deburring than another of the same brand name and type sold in a different store of the same name.

Zinc plated chain should not be stored in contact with dissimilar metals. The interaction of the two different metals can cause one or both of them to have a corrosive effect especially if there is any water present. This effect might be able to be remediated by use of white vinegar but in the worst case it will be permanent. The interaction between zinc-plated chain and connectors made of other materials is completely safe in a dry environment and does not suffer any extreme side effects from human sweat either.

In general the finish for zinc-plated can be cleaned and "refreshed" with a white vinegar bath and a water rinse followed by total drying. However, do not let the chain sit in vinegar because that will oxidize the finish as well, and affect the feel and appearance.

Plastic

Plastic chain is an excellent material to make a choice on whether or not chain bondage is for you. It is cheap per foot sold and comes in a variety of sizes and colors. It photographs great and is practical for developing and exploring ideas for bondage harnesses and positions. It tolerates a wide variety of environmental conditions: it can get wet, warm, cold, and dried and it will not change its properties very much outside of extreme treatments (fire, liquid nitrogen, etc.) There is a reason that it is used outdoors extensively to mark pathways.

An end of a plastic chain length. Note the lack of finishing details: sharp edges, burrs.

Unfortunately it has a lot of downsides; this is a literal case of you get what you pay for. For one, plastic chain doesn't provide the same sensation that metallic chain does. The feeling of heft, of weighted constraint, doesn't apply. Plastic chain does not have as smooth of a finish as metal chain and that could be a distraction during the bondage scene. There is a chance that the finish may even be unpleasant as there isn't a lot of time spent in the finishing process during manufacturing in order to keep costs down.

While it does exist in different sizes there are a lot of "non-standard" sizes available on the market.

This means that you will probably have difficulties finding plastic chain in big box stores that will allow you to use any connectors that you purchase, even if the plastic chain is listed as being the same size as those connectors.

You can order plastic chain on-line, but you will have to verify the size with the manufacturer/supplier to be sure that it is suitable for the types of connectors you will want to use. If you verify the size of the chain in advance you can use any connector you would like.

In the event that you still want to experiment with plastic chain without spending additional money on metal connectors, you can fabricate a basic plastic connector by cutting individual links in two places to form an open link to join longer plastic chain lengths together. Normally we would not recommend using open connectors, but **remember: plastic chain is more decorative than anything else. It will not hold someone in bondage as securely as you might want and is not load bearing under any circumstances.**

Despite the disadvantages, plastic chain is cheap enough to order to gauge how well you like chain bondage. At time of printing, the cost is generally under or around US $1.00/foot.

Other Finishes

Chain is also available in powder-coated or painted finishes, but those run the risk of surface damage under stress and use, revealing an unsuitable surface for bondage underneath. These coatings may also be less safe for human contact, since the chain is coated to protect it from environmental damage. This chain may not be able to be cleaned in the same way as stainless or zinc-plated. Stainless steel, plastic, and zinc-plated are accepted to be non-toxic to humans and we advise people to keep bondage that way!

You might see chains and connectors that are "galvanized". While it is priced well, you do not want to purchase this style of hardware. It has a very rough finish and does not handle well nor does it feel good against the skin. It does not have a "pretty" surface finish. It is not satisfactory for bondage.

Chain Maintenance

Any respectable Top performs routine inspection and maintenance of their toys. Chain is no exception to this but it is especially true because checking for premature failure or manufacturing defects should be a regular priority in order to maintain a good record of safety. A Bottom being damaged from a chain bondage scene due to negligence is a terrible sin indeed, as it could have been avoided.

Part of routine inspection and maintenance involves cleaning your chain regularly and checking for burrs. It also means checking chain for surface damage, irregular wear, cracks, breaks, or change in size or shape of chain links. Any of these could mean that the chain might be nearing or at a point of mechanical failure, and should be replaced.

In general, your chain will have a good shelf life as long as it is maintained well, stored in a dry place where it is not affected by moisture, and not stored in contact with dissimilar metals. There is no right or wrong container to store chain as long as it meets that criteria. We prefer to store our chain in a big red plastic bucket attached to a rolling cart designed to move up and down stairs. It turns out that when you have many different lengths of chain (upwards of 100 feet) it starts to become unwieldy and heavy. Moving it becomes a challenge when taking it to locations and the way you store it will be critical. Store it in the best way that accommodates the way you work best, however that manifests itself.

It is important to note that along with the physical care comes challenges to transporting it to different locations. We have not yet had the opportunity to attempt to fly anywhere or take a train trip with all of our chain bondage equipment. It has traveled mostly on car road trips which works pretty well minus having to be concerned about the rear suspension of my vehicle when I put it in the trunk. For the record, I drive a smallish hatchback. Your mileage may vary.

Chain Specifications

When you get to buying your first chain, all the different selections in a store or online can be overwhelming if you do not understand what to look for. The style of chain we use in this book is generally classified by "Grade", which also has a corresponding name:

- Grade 30 - "Proof Coil"
- Grade 43 - "High Test"
- Grade 70 - "Transport"
- Grade 80 - "Alloy"
- Grade 100 - also "Alloy", for some reason.

The Grade number is a general indicator of its maximum stress at its ultimate strength or tensile strength. Tensile strength is the ability of a material to withstand forces pulling it apart in opposite directions.

Another key factor to look out for is the Working Load Limit or WLL, sometimes called Safe Working Limit or SWL. In the US this is typically listed as a number in pounds meaning that you should try to not exceed the WLL of any given chain or connector whatsoever. For our purposes the WLL of 1/4" Zinc-Plated Grade 30 Proof Coil chain is around 1300 pounds. This is a far greater force than any person could exceed in order to explosively "break free" from chain bondage, but is relatively small considering Grade 100 Alloy chain links of the same size generally have a WLL of 4300 pounds. This is twice the weight of some small cars, equivalent to the curb weight of some Ford F150 pick-up trucks or about a thousand pounds more than a Subaru WRX, plus or minus 200 pounds.

Lastly, chain size will be of a significant consideration to you as it will maximize (or limit) the types and sizes of connectors available for you to use in your chain bondage journey. It will also affect the way you will be able to handle and manipulate the chain before and after it is on your Bottom.

Chain is measured in four dimensions as shown: the inside length (A), inside width (B), link width (C), and wire size (D). The most critical of these dimensions relative to our purposes are the wire size, and the inside length. The inside length will determine what types of devices you can put inside of a chain link in addition to the existing link(s). If the inside length is not at least three times the wire size plus a little bit extra you will have a hard time using connectors and devices in this method of chain bondage.

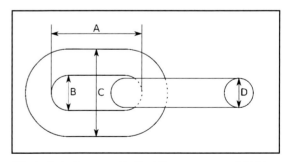

Chain link diagram. Dotted lines represent hidden features. The weld in the link is not featured.

We have found that 1/4" chain handles the best, has a reasonable WLL for our risk profiles, does not overwhelm the Bottom in terms of weight on the body, and has a reasonable amount of connectors available to use though we specifically tend to limit ourselves to just a few types of them in order to not overwhelm our process. **From here onward the phrases, "Proof Coil Chain", "Zinc-Plated", or "Regular" all refer to 1/4" Grade 30 Zinc-Plated Proof Coil Chain, with a WLL of 1300 pounds.** This is what will be used in demonstration and example photographs.

Chain Connections

So far, a lot of what has been written covers the chain itself and only peppers the concept of connectors throughout the text. The time has come to share the other significant part of the chain bondage equation.

The connectors outlined in this section are what we feel are the best to work with in terms of simplicity, capability, and flexibility in terms of use.

Before continuing it is necessary to have a quick mention of safety, ratings, and our risk profile. In all of our hardware we have assumed a 4:1 or 5:1 safety factor. Cecilia weighs about 200 pounds, and many of the connectors we are about to describe have a WLL of 800 pounds or more. 800 / 200 = 4. Typically having a higher safety factor is better.

What does this actually mean in terms of our risk profile? A larger ratio means a greater peace of mind to us. We feel that having a margin of four or five times as much force that can be applied to cause a connector failure is reasonable. You will have to determine what you feel comfortable with. We are not going to dictate that there is "one true way" or "one true safety factor" for the sake of the bondage illustrated in this book. If you do not accept anything at or below a 5:1 safety factor, then consider hardware made with different materials.

Anchor Shackles

The premier device in chain bondage is the screw pin anchor shackle ("shackle"). This is the Swiss army knife of chain bondage in terms of keeping things together. It is a two-piece device: a threaded screw pin with a tab for twisting and a shaped piece of metal that is flattened, drilled through, and threaded on one side for the screw pin to interface with. There is an "open" side and a "threaded" side.

1/4" Stainless Steel Screw Pin Anchor Shackle. Pin is in the open position. In this instance, the "threaded" side is on the left part of the shackle.

Pin is in the closed position. The hole is present for securing closed with wire. The "open" side is facing you, the reader.

A significant advantage that screw pin anchor shackles have for bondage use is that they don't require any external tools to use. They can be quickly attached and detached if necessary. They can also be unscrewed under tension by hand with a little bit of effort. This allows you to be able to get your Bottom out of bondage faster than using bolt cutters or other tools, which will be discussed later.

A disadvantage is that they do require two-hand operation. If you are able to open and close an anchor shackle fully with one hand, there are lots of people who would probably be interested in your dexterity.

Shackles can also be secured using wire without any permanent alteration to the device making it very unlikely to become disassembled for a long time. In this configuration the screw pin is intended to be connected in a more permanent way. Usually you might find these in places where safety is critical but it takes tools to wire it up or release it if necessary. If you are looking for psychological play in your chain bondage this may be an option for you.

A regular (non-anchor) screw pin shackle wired shut.

Anchor shackles have a good loading capacity relative to the sizes available. They can also be acquired for a decent cost but do fall under the "consumable" part of your budget for bondage. It is possible that they can wear out over time through excessive or "shock" loading where the force applied to the connector is instantaneous.

They are available in a wide variety of finishes but in continuing with hardware recommendations we suggest **1/4" stainless steel screw pin anchor shackles**. If you buy them from a manufacturer that certifies their WLL rating you will pay a little bit of a premium, but that does come with an amount of assumed safety. They are available "generically" and might have a certain WLL rating but be aware that it could be less than what it is stamped with. The shackles we typically use are rated for a claimed 800 - 1000 pounds WLL.

Anchor shackles have a lot of flexibility in the way they can be used with some limitations. The orientation of the shackle is somewhat critical in their use which may allow you to quickly disassemble the bondage if you plan well enough in advance. Ideally shackles should be loaded in an in-line fashion with one chain link connected to the screw pin and the other(s) connected 180 degrees apart on the bow. However, an anchor shackle *can* be loaded in different directions with a decrease in the amount of the WLL depending on the load directions.

There may be situations where loading in an in-line way is not ideal. It is totally okay to do it, as long as you do not exceed the WLL while loading in those directions.

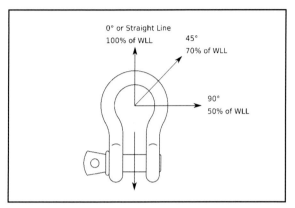

WLL Diagram for screw pin anchor shackles. This diagram does not apply to any other shackle type you might find on the market.

Chain segments attached in an "in-line" fashion to an anchor shackle. The bow of the shackle is on the left. The pin cannot hold more than one link.

It is our preference to use shackles in-line as much as possible in order to maximize the capability of them. "Side-loading" (loading in a perpendicular fashion) reduces the capacity in which they can be loaded, and thus become a faster consumable if accidentally or intentionally overloaded.

Exceeding the WLL will cause deformation of the anchor shackle and depending on how it has been loaded, the deformation can be specific. Catastrophic failure is unlikely when being used for bondage barring some serious manufacturing defect or falsified specification, but the shackle can **plastically deform** never to return back to the original shape. One way that it can be deformed by exceeding WLL is through "necking" of the shackle screw pin. This will cause it to 'look weird' (technical term), relative to an undeformed shackle pin, and is cause for concern.

The image to the right shows an undeformed shackle (top) and a deformed one (bottom). The necking of the screw pin on the bottom shackle can be seen near the threaded portion (left), while the top screw pin is in good physical shape. For clarification the shackle with the necked pin is marked.

If any of the pins of your shackles reach this state consider replacing the shackle.

The shackle bow itself can also deform but as long as the deformation is minor and occurs with the pin attached and fully screwed in, the deformation is less likely to affect the functionality of the shackle unless the shape change is extreme either instantaneously or over a period of time. It might make the shackle harder to use especially when some circumstances might call for it to be repositioned while under tension. It also may cause the chain to lie atypically against a Bottom's skin.

Because some variance exists in the manufacture of anchor shackles the deformation could mean that the pin that goes with that particular shackle and the shackle itself are now permanently married to each other, and the task of maintaining their monogamous relationship might be an extra item to mentally keep track of. That shackle and pin cannot swing with others.

In addition to proper loading there are also optimal and less optimal ways to connect multiple shackles together. The rounded shape of the bow provides a small area on the inside of the arch where a shackle will best interface. This area is at the top of the arch of the bow if you're looking at a shackle with the same orientation as the WLL diagram on the previous page. This is the most optimal place to connect shackles to other connectors. It ensures a contact area with the least amount of slip between two different round features: the arch of the bow, and the rounded interior of the chain link itself (round-to-round). Round-to-round is the best way to make a connection because there is very little opportunity for the connection to slip or move under tension.

The second optimal way to connect a shackle to a chain link or another connector is round-to-cylinder. This means attaching the pin of the shackle to another round feature: to a chain link or another shackle bow, for example. In this case you still gain the benefit of a small contact area in the bow of the shackle, but it interfaces with a cylindrical face which might allow slipping along the shaft. This may be less desired because it allows for minor shifting of the connection to occur under tension.

In the example to the left, from top to bottom there is a round-to-round connection made between the chain and the bow of the shackle; there is a round-to-cylinder connection made between the top shackle and the lower shackle, and there is a round-to-cylinder connection made between the lower shackle and the chain link at the bottom. The only points where there can be slippage are between the chain at the bottom and the lower shackle, and the lower shackle and the top shackle.

In the configuration to the right, from top to bottom there is a round-to-cylinder connection between the top shackle and the top chain; a round-to-round connection between the upper and lower shackle, and a round-to-cylinder connection between the lower shackle and the lower chain link. The places where slipping may occur are between the top chain and top shackle, and between the lower chain and the lower shackle. Because the connection made between the two shackles is round-to-round, under tension this would be a stable configuration. It would be unlikely to shift at all between the two shackles even with the two round-to-cylinder connections at the top and bottom.

The configuration to the left is the least optimal one because of the cylinder-to-cylinder connection made in the middle. While there are good round-to-round connections between the top shackle/top chain and bottom shackle/bottom chain, there is a tremendous amount of slip and rotation that can occur between the two shackles in the middle. A good analogy of this type of connection would be to think of a ball joint.

Another disadvantage of this configuration is that it is also the hardest to perform if you have limited room to work with. Because of the geometry of shackles, they do not go together trivially in this way. There is some spatial manipulation required to get the shackles in this position, but this leads to another issue: they will not come apart immediately under tension just by unscrewing the pins. The ends of the shackle are almost in an interlocking orientation that prevents fast release, and in an emergency this might not be ideal to help your Bottom out of the bondage as necessary.

There may be times in which this configuration is useful, such as when there are multiple chain links that need to be connected to both bows of both shackles and you know that the overall connection will have a fair amount of tension, as will be shown in a chest harness later on. In cases like these you will have to consider alternate plans for the quick release of the bondage.

Quick Links

Quick links are a classic example of a connector used in just about any chain application but they do have some restrictions when used in chain bondage. They are a single piece of combined hardware having a loop and a long nut, and are designed to resemble a chain link. They have the ability to be opened or closed with one hand by twisting the nut or permanently closed through material deformation using tools.

When quick links are used in bondage they can make connections between lengths of chain look almost totally seamless for better aesthetics.

Quick link in the closed state, with the nut up against the shoulder of the thread.

Quick link in the open state. The distance in the gap is a part of its size measurement.

While most screw pin anchor shackles used for bondage reliably operate in the same way with minor cosmetic differences, some quick links are manufactured differently much to the detriment of their functionality--despite looking and operating exactly the same way. This unfortunate distinction has to do with the way the threaded nut is allowed to travel along the thread.

The quick link to the right in the photo (stainless) is manufactured with a shoulder that prevents the nut from moving further by hand. The quick link to the left (zinc-plated, oxidized) is manufactured with a collar that allows the nut to travel over the top of it.

Depending on how the manufacturer produced the link you could end up in a situation where hand tightening of the nut cannot be easily undone and might require a tool. When shopping for quick links pay attention to the way the nut is allowed to close and open and the size of the opening to make sure it will work with your chain.

In the first photo the two quick links are mostly closed. In the second photo both quick links are tightened using finger tightness but the nut on the upper-right quick link has moved beyond the collar *just enough* to not be able to be opened by hand anymore.

The lower-left quick link has a curved shoulder that prevents the nut from being over tightened without a tool and deformed as a result. The upper-right quick link has a collar that allows the nut to slip over with only finger tightening.

Both links have their nut moved to the fully closed position. The lower quick link has been hand tightened fully and will not advance further. The upper was able to be advanced a tiny amount with very little effort that it cannot be opened by hand.

While use of the quick link is less complex, the limitation is that it can only be disconnected from bondage when the link is no longer under tension. To remove it, the chain has to be able to rotate along the wire of the link until it reaches the open position. Quick links must always remain closed while in tension during bondage in order to avoid failure. Never perform bondage with a quick link left in its open state. Never load a quick link in any other direction than what it is intended for. They cannot be side-loaded.

As usual, they come in different sizes and finishes and so **1/4" stainless steel quick links with a WLL of 1000 pounds are recommended**. You may have to do a bit of searching to find them with this criteria including the specific closure of the nut as they are a very cheap, mass produced connector.

If you cannot find quick links that you are satisfied with they can be substituted with an anchor shackle.

Quick Releases

Quick releases are devices that can be operated with one hand and offer a way to keep a device closed with very little movement to open it back up in case of an emergency. Sometimes these are also known as "panic snaps", or "panic releases", for this reason. The method of release is also designed to be *not accidental*.

They come in different mechanical fashions with some being better for our purposes than others.

An advantage of quick releases is that they can be opened under tension. They can also be load bearing but sometimes the data about the amount of load they can withstand is not available. This should be taken into account when considering their use and placement.

Quick releases usually have one openable end and one fixed closed end. This means that quick releases actually require the use of two connectors. One end attaches to a chain link, and the other which requires a connector to attach to a link. This will affect your chain bondage budget. If you intend to use these anywhere consider that before you put bondage on your Bottom.

These are available in stainless and can be compatible with 1/4" chain. They are somewhat specialized and can take a little more shopping around to find them. They are not readily found in big box hardware stores. As a result of their design and specialized functionality they run a premium in price, usually more than US $10 per unit.

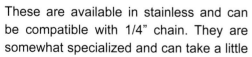

Rings

It may be that when you are making a lot of connections in one location you may end up crowding or overloading a single shackle with different connections that are tensioned in multiple directions. This can be avoided with proficient chain bondage design but sometimes it is easier to use a linking ring or other solid, welded geometric piece to make your design happen.

 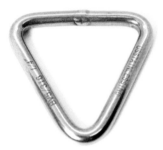

These are all referred to as 'rings' despite having shapes that do not imply perfect roundness. Rings come in different shapes with different finishes and breaking load ratings.

Generally, you want to find a ring size that isn't too large or too small to work with that has a very high breaking load strength of thousands of pounds.

The WLL of these rings is the breaking load divided by some safety factor. In the example of the O-ring shown the breaking load is 5900 pounds. If we assume a 10:1 safety factor the WLL will be 590 pounds which is more than a good enough rating for our risk profile. In the example of the triangle ring, the breaking load is 4400 pounds. Assuming 10:1 safety factor the WLL is 440 pounds.

The material diameter of the rings we use is not 1/4" (smaller is okay), but the specifications are sufficient for our purposes. They also look good aesthetically and let us accomplish our bondage objectives. They are available in 316 stainless steel and can be found for under US $10 per unit.

Though rings are useful for combining a lot of ends with connectors at a point, they are not perfect at keeping those connectors in an exact orientation. The connectors may move around a little, which is important to consider in their use when building harnesses and using rings as an attachment point for other segments. If you are able to keep good tension in the segments, that will serve the rest of the bondage better.

One way to give yourself an advantage when using shackles with rings is to be sure that the bow of the shackle is the place where it attaches to a ring when the shackle will be under tension. This forces two geometrically round objects to constrain themselves to a smaller contact area. If you connect the shackle and ring together at the pin side, then there is an opportunity for the shackle to rotate in an albeit limited but unwanted way. This could also cause the chain to shift around slightly which may cause further issues with tension in the bondage.

A final advantage of using rings is that they minimize the opportunity for side loading, premature wear, and deformation of connectors. You do not have to use them but they do become useful in specific cases as we will demonstrate with some harness variations later on.

Connectors to Avoid

There are some bad choices in connectors that are unfortunately ubiquitous in the alternative lifestyle.

One of these is the snap hook. You will see them on leashes, collars, cuffs, St. Andrew's Crosses, or other attachment hardware. They have an extremely limited WLL; sometimes as little as One (1) pound. They are spring operated with an exposed notch where the spring can be affected by water or other environmental conditions causing the spring to get stuck or to fail completely.

Snap hooks are possibly injurious depending on the intensity of the spring used to close the plunger. They can pinch skin very easily and are not often well machined.

Keychain Rings and keychain carabiners are also connectors to avoid. On the packaging it will usually say "NOT FOR CLIMBING", "NOT WEIGHT BEARING", or other similar language. Although you will find that every connector and chain available for purchase will say things like "Not for Overhead Lifting" or "Not for Use on Humans," we willfully disregard those as a part of our risk profile because of the WLL

rating. Connectors and chain that have a significantly small WLL or no WLL we take at their word as a matter of life and death.

Any open connector should also be avoided. This means S-hooks, eye bolts, some swivels, or any other connector made from wire-drawn metal that is not fully closed and or lacks a securing mechanism. It might be enticing to use them because of their cost and ease of use but you exchange that for personal safety and high risk to health.

Non-Chain Related Devices

There are lots of things you can connect to chain that aren't specifically meant for chain hardware even though they are compatible with the size of chain that we use throughout this book. Some of our favorites are listed here.

Cuffs

Ankle cuffs and wrist cuffs offer places to attach chains and connectors with a reasonably strong piece of hardware on them. Usually the attachment point is a D-ring, O-ring, or Triangle.

There are a few recommendations when buying cuffs. The first is that fabric cuffs, "sex shop cuffs", fuzzy cuffs, or cuffs made of other thin material are not appropriate for chain bondage. This also includes novelty or other "play handcuffs". You get exactly what you pay for in this department. If it looks cheap it is cheap and will not sustain bondage activity for very long. They are decorative at best. They are good if you want to look kinky but are hesitant to participate in bondage.

We recommend cuffs made of either thick leather or other metal hardware. Leather is a good material because it has some flex, but also good strength and reasonable comfort. Fuzzy, padded leather cuffs exist but be aware that they may slide around on the skin more which would be unwanted.

Metal cuffs--non-law enforcement handcuffs--offer no such give. They might be very sturdy but there is usually no way to adjust the size or comfort and may cause wear on the skin over time. There is certainly an aesthetic in metal cuffs though which cannot be understated.

When buying a pair or a set of cuffs pay close attention to the way the cuffs are manufactured. Do the buckles appear sturdy? Do the sizing holes have grommets in them to prevent unnecessary wear and tear over time? Is there additional velcro attached to help cuff placement and securing? How is the sizing band attached to the cuff--is it glued, held together with a screw and nut, or both? Are there lots of stitches keeping the cuffs together, or fewer larger stitches? There's a phrase you should be aware of: "Cry once; buy once." With cuffs you get what you pay for.

Wide band cuffs are generally better than skinny band cuffs because they spread out any forces applied to a joint where the cuffs will cover. The ideal leather cuffs should also have two opposing attachment points on them whether they are D-rings or O-rings.

A vinyl wrist and ankle cuff. A number of studs keep them together and the attachment point is an O-ring that pulls evenly on a triangle ring.

Cuffs made of vinyl or PVC can be sufficient as long as they are thick and sturdy. We have some experience with them for doing chain bondage in water but that is a higher risk of activity than we feel comfortable discussing in this book.

We do not recommend alternative or "vegan leather" style cuffs as the wearability of the material over time is not great. Vegan leather is made of polymers, is usually thinner, cannot be conditioned to improve wear over time, and suffers mechanical breakdown in the material because it is made from plastics. Vegan leather is also made from non-renewable sources and has a larger negative environmental impact.

Spreader Bars

There are a lot of different spreader bars out on the market all made by different people with different materials. They can be used in chain bondage as long as the mounts on either end of the bar are strong enough to not mechanically fail when used. Ideally the ends of the spreader bar should have a solid D- or O-ring, or other type of shackle. If your spreader bar has something other than a ring or shackle at the ends make sure to be careful about the kinds of forces you apply.

Be sure that the connections at the ends of the spreader bar also have enough clearance for the types of connectors you would like to use on them. In our case the spreader bar allows the quick release, the quick link, and the pin of the anchor shackle to be attached to the eye bolt. As a spreader bar falls under 'novelties', specifications are likely not available for the construction of it so use caution when making decisions about how to use it.

Insertables with Attachment Points

There are some penetrative "sex toys" (anal hooks, other insertables with rings, etc.) in the market that have an attachment place for devices to connect to. You can integrate them into your bondage scene though it is advised to not rely on that device to keep your bondage together. Consider it more of an addition rather than a focused feature. Don't build the bondage around the adult novelties.

A word of caution on anal hooks: they have their own set of risks that may not be outlined on or in the packaging. Use them at your own risk. Discussion of health risks due to adult novelty toys is not covered in this book but there are plenty of sources available if you choose to seek them out. Consider asking your medical professional friends for any stories they might have about things "found" inside other humans. These are usually good examples of tragic humor, or tales of desperate misery.

Spring Clips & Carabiners

Spring clips and carabiners are looped devices that feature a spring pinned hinge on a gate that closes the loop. They are another single piece of hardware and are sold in both hardware and outdoor enthusiast stores. The ones sold in hardware and rigging supply stores are usually more industrial looking, while the ones sold in outdoor enthusiast stores are usually colored; flashy; lighter-weight; made from strong, weight-saving materials, and have the specifications printed right on them.

This carabiner has a simple wire loop as a spring loaded gate. It is marked with a rating.

This works the same as a carabiner, but is called a spring clip. Why? We have no idea.

These devices are all pretty similar in functionality with some notable exceptions. Some of these devices come with a special locking feature that involves a threaded cylinder that screws to close over the interface between the loop and the gate that prevents it from opening accidentally.

These come in another version in which the locking cylinder is spring loaded at the locking position and must be retracted to open the carabiner.

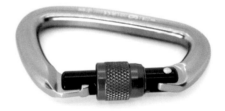

A locking carabiner.

In some of these devices, there is a partial operating risk to the Top. Specifically on spring clips there often exists a very poorly finished piece at the end of the gate that could be a pinching/injury hazard if care is not taken when using the connector. An advantage that the carabiners for climbing have over the ones designed for chain is that the gate is not nearly as hazardous, likely due to the intent for climbing carabiners to not be able to damage rope lines they will be attached to. They are not explicitly designed to be used with chain as a primary function, but they can be found in appropriate sizes and strengths required.

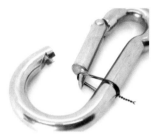  

The spring gate doesn't require much force to use or to keep open...

...but use caution to make sure you don't snap the gate on your finger/hand.

Note the rounded gate and the cylindrical stop. These may pinch but they won't bite!

The other main difference is that the ones designed for use with chain are usually made of a material that has a circular diameter. You may find that the carabiners sold in outdoor enthusiast stores limit rotation in the chain link because the dimension of the loop is larger in one direction than it is in another. The fact that the carabiners that are designed for for use with chain are not limited in their movement is the reason why they might be more readily used for bondage.

They all function in the same way in terms of a spring loaded gate, so for some it's a preference of style and movement within a chain link. The carabiners sold in outdoor enthusiast stores can be perfectly serviceable as long as this is kept in mind. As long as they are compatible with the existing chain used and range of motion isn't an issue, it is entirely up to you which you want to employ.

These connectors are also only properly used while the tension is in-line with the gate. They cannot be released until tension is removed. In some cases tension will also not permit the gate to open (even if it is NOT a locking carabiner), so it will not be able to be forced open. Forcing open a carabiner is not a trivial feat. Do not attempt to load these connectors in any other direction than they are intended for.

These are available in other finishes than stainless steel but we prefer them in stainless. The size you want to look out for is 1/4", but pay attention to the WLL as well. It's possible that these connectors may not be available in 1000 pound WLL in the desired finish. If using carabiners pay attention to the force limit designed in kiloNewtons (kN). Generally higher is better but make sure that it fits with the chain you're using.

The prices can vary wildly from type and store.

Locks

Locks are an unfortunate staple of bondage in general. They are featured in chastity devices, restraints, adult outerwear… the applications in kink are pretty endless if you are creative. They deserve a brief mention here though.

There is a wild range of design in the world of padlocks, which means that every lock shank or shackle has a different specification for the strength of that part. This is because there is no "accepted standard" of what the tensile strength of a padlock should be. There is no "perfect" padlock, which means that they are all susceptible to different kinds of attacks implying that the mode of failure is also different from lock to lock. **It is up to you whether or not you choose to accept the possible accidental structural failure of a lock in your chain bondage scene.** If that is a part of your risk profile then the only suggestion that can be provided is to avoid putting the padlock in a key structural place of the bondage on your Bottom.

There is no justification to suggest that a padlock will be suitable for bondage. In addition to the aforementioned failures of locks there have been many, many tales about lost keys. The amount of time you will need to undo a padlock in the event of an emergency should also be a deterrent especially if they are not keyed the same.

Safety

Any bondage is a high-risk activity as previously mentioned in Chapter Two. Many of the risks have been outlined but there are a few related specifically to the chain bondage experience.

The first is somewhat counter-intuitive. Bolt cutters are not the most effective tool to release someone out of bondage in an emergency. Sounds wrong, right? A chain link has to be cut in two places in order to free someone, and one of those places will be right next to the Bottom's skin which significantly increases the risk of an injury. Additionally, the physical strength needed to cut chain links is very high and good leverage won't always be an option. If you are a chain bondage Top with lesser explosive strength, operating a bolt cutter may not be in your best interest.

A much better choice is to loosen a connector whether that be an anchor shackle, quick release, or any other connector suggested in this book. In the event that the connector is stuck or cannot be turned, a good pair of pliers will be more effective at releasing it. This is a rare occurrence as long as you maintain proper storage and care of your hardware. If a connector is hard to unfasten it can also be that you have improperly positioned or tensioned a connector in a way that makes it hard to operate. You may have to remove tension elsewhere first, or the connector may be wearing out.

If a connector is hard to open or close (jams), consider inspecting it for any faults or deformations that might affect its safety or operation and discard it if necessary.

Reversing the order of bondage put on a Bottom may not be the best course of action either since there is an implicit order of assembly of some harnesses and predicaments. Through good planning and use of connectors bondage can be released at major intersection points. It can technically be released anywhere but if the arms are restrained and required to be used first in a hurry, not releasing the bondage restricting them initially won't be helpful to the emergency. This should make more sense in some of the examples later on.

In the event of a non-life threatening, minor emergency, a well-stocked first aid kit can suffice for any other physical issues that come up.

Alright... Where Do I Buy This Stuff?

Now that we've covered mostly everything you would need to know in terms of hardware, here are the places we prefer to source those items from.

Chain

We found that the best place to acquire chain with very little questions asked is from big box home improvement stores. You can buy it in bulk from a rigging supplier, or online, but be aware you may pay shipping costs and you will need a way to cut it which was very briefly covered under "Chain Materials", the first section of this chapter.

If you're buying plastic chain to try it out, you should definitely buy it online. Shipping will be cheap as will be the product. Plastic chains sold in big box stores may be limited in selection, size, and color.

You can also buy chain from farm supply stores or independent hardware stores that are in rural areas with varying degrees of selection and price. At this time we do not recommend "discount" hardware or freight stores as the quality and selection of products that you will need that they sell isn't assured. We also do not recommend marine supply stores or catalogues as the upcharges are enormous due to the fact that they are already catering to people who own boats--a money-pit lifestyle hobby in and of itself.

Connectors

The best place to buy connectors is from rigging supply outfits, although you will have to make sure that they sell to the public. Don't buy them from big box retail stores because the upcharge is really high for the amount of them you will need. Two to four dollars (at time of writing) versus five or more dollars per connector will add up quickly when you start buying them in bulk. Rigging supply outfits may even be able to offer them at a discount where applicable. They are used to selling this kind of equipment regularly so you generally don't have to worry about telling them that you're going to use it for some kinky bondage. You should only disclose what you are comfortable revealing. Calling it a project is okay.

Rigging suppliers will also have an informed opinion about the type of connectors you are buying as well as where the connectors are made. Take their assessment at face value as it plays into your risk profile regarding the capability of the hardware you are acquiring.

Farm supply stores usually have a decent selection of connectors as well in the finishes that you want, but the price may differ. Sometimes these stores will have the odd type of connector that you are seeking in the finish that you desire, which is an interesting experience because going to buy equipment with the intent of using it for sexy bondage times at a place that also sells horse feed might cause you to have a double take. We have had to acquire some of the connectors we use this way, often driving more than an hour out of the way to get exactly what we wanted.

You can also buy them online but the price will vary wildly for what you want, in the quantity you want, and for the quality you're looking for. We again do not recommend discount, freight, or marine supply stores, even if they have online retail channels.

Cuffs, Insertables, Spreader Bars, etc.

When you're buying adult novelty specialties consider supporting your independently owned local sex supply store first. If you decide to save a few bucks or are not satisfied with what you can get locally, you will probably be able to contact a vendor directly to get a custom order made. The advantage is that you might be able to get something specifically designed for a good price, or even at a discount if they're trying to liquidate some of their inventory. You can also get questions answered about the usability/wearability of their products better than you would at a store.

Vending events, e.g. kinky "Flea Markets," (depending on where you're from) are a good place to talk to vendors and see a wide variety of products for sale at various prices. These are also good places to try things on to see how well they fit or how well they are made before buying. Sometimes the vendors will have specials running during the event and you can get their wares at a discount.

The non-commercial non-industrial market for sex accessories is very informal with each vendor relying on their own way to make, sell, and distribute product. Sometimes local stores that have very knowledgeable staff who can make good recommendations exist, and it is a good idea to consult them if they have contacts with custom makers and suppliers. Don't be afraid to ask around.

Cost

We would be remiss if we did not briefly mention the upfront cost of all of the hardware we have purchased. There are a few points to be made first.

First is that we did not acquire all of the equipment overnight and we suggest you do not either. We found that as we enjoyed What It Is That We Do (WIITWD), we wanted to do bigger and more interesting shapes and scenes, so acquiring all of our hardware was a stepwise, multi-year investment.

Second, chain bondage hardware is durable and will last a long time if you take care of it, lasting years depending on wear and tear. Things that are considered consumables are connectors as they will likely wear out faster than the chain you acquire. Those will eventually have to be replaced, which is a smaller percentage of what you will be paying overall. Having to replace parts of your bondage kit from regular activity would be true for any other bondage medium.

Third, if this becomes something you are passionate about, it will evolve into a thing between a hobby and a lifestyle which never comes for free. You will want to evaluate what it is you want to accomplish and so setting goals will be important to determine what you are willing to spend. Collectively we own over 100 feet of Zinc-plated chain, 48 shackles (10 retired as of this writing), two quick releases, six quick links, a few spring clips/carabiners, two sets of leather wrist and ankle cuffs, and a spreader bar, with a bulk of the cost being the leather cuffs. We made every attempt to buy at a non-retail price, but your experience may differ.

Creating Your First Kit

There are a few things you should think about when acquiring your first bondage kit. The first is whether or not you will be performing bondage on one person or on multiple people. You will likely want to acquire at least one length of chain that can go twice around the widest area of the hips, or torso and arms, of a larger body type. For some of the designs shown later on, you will need two identical lengths that fit around an average to larger sized torso and arms. It will also benefit you to purchase other lengths that can fit twice around an average thigh. You will probably need some shorter lengths to connect segments together, but this amount of chain may vary depending on the kinds of designs you would like to make.

Recall that for this book, we use 1/4" zinc-plated chain and hardware for all of the examples shown. If you choose to use other sized chains and hardware, you may have to accommodate for the different size, or some of the examples may not work for you at all. Make sure that the chain you acquire has the correct 3:1 ratio of inside width to chain link wire width. You should be able to fit a connector in between the two adjacent chain links. Confirm that any devices you fantasize about using with chain can connect with shackles or other connectors that you buy.

A recommended number of shackles for starting out is three per chain segment. You will see later that the beginning chain bondage shapes can use up to three shackles to build.

Chapter 4 - The How

We're almost at the point of showing techniques! But there's a bit more theory to discuss. This *is about doing the bondage* though, so we're not far off. In Chapter One considerations were presented when thinking about the lengths of chains that might be required to put on a person. Now that you know what hardware to look out for you can start thinking about putting that into practice, with a few minor additions.

We want to reiterate the disclaimer, that **anything that is shown in this book is only to be performed at <u>YOUR OWN RISK.</u> Bondage can be a dangerous activity and the techniques shown going forward are performed under the assumption that you are choosing to participate in this activity under your own cognizance and consent. You assume responsibility for anything that causes harm to yourself, another person, property, being, creature, or any other thing that exists that hasn't been mentioned. These techniques have not been vetted by any agency, manufacturer, body, association, or individual as being safe.**

In order to describe how to put chain on a person we need to define a few terms. These terms will help to convey the ideas in the following sections that cover different aspects of chain bondage-- some practical, some theoretical.

A **Budget** refers to the total amount of hardware you have, sometimes specifically referring to the amount of connectors available. If something is "expensive", it requires a lot of your available hardware.

A **Wrap** is a single closed loop of chain that might or might not have slack at the closed point. It is a part of a single column.

A **Single Column** (or **column**) is two or more wraps of chain around one part of the body, e.g. an arm, a leg, a waist, a chest, a torso, etc.

A **Double Column** is a wrap around two parts of the body that keeps them physically together, but also distinct usually referencing two arms, two legs, or two thighs. The part that keeps them distinct is a bridge between two parts of the body. This definition is not limited to two of the same body part.

A **Harness** is a combination of chain and connectors on a body that facilitates a function, e.g. a chest harness, or a hip harness.

Reverse Tension is tension applied in the opposite direction from the way the initial wrap was placed on the body.

The **Common Link** refers to the chain link where a direction change occurs and the link is rotated in such a way that establishes intent of direction for the slack.

The chain link between the shackle and the rest of the length of chain is the common link, which has the shackle connection on the right, and two chain links on the left.

The position of the common link in a single column on a thigh.

Having the ability to form common links is one of the most important skills in chain bondage. They guide the flow of the bondage in the right direction and help you to manage leftover slack. In the example shown to the right there is tension applied on both sides of the shackle. The chain is flowing in a direction from the shackle in a wrap traveling along the lower chain to a reverse tension on the upper chain, and the link attached to the bow is rotated so that the reverse tension is directed in an unobstructed way.

One way to think about the common link orientation is that if it is being used in a reverse tension, you want the upper link attached to the common link to compress against the lower link attached to the common link to hold the lower link in place. Part of the common link's function is also to make sure to keep any reverse tensions applied as closely together as possible.

Method

As you'll see in the following how-to sections most of the bondage applied includes double wraps for single columns, with or without slack. This is because they are more comfortable than a single wrap and creates more sustainable bondage. Make sure you consider bodily measurements of your Bottom twice.

Early in our journey we did bondage with just a single wrap. While this was fine for decorative and less functional bondage, it was limiting for longer and more sophisticated scenes. Single wraps under tension were extremely uncomfortable and often scene ending before the entire bondage design could be completed. Sometimes single line attachments are okay because they aren't creating discomfort on the body. This will be shown in some harnesses.

Tension

Tension in bondage doesn't exist in a vacuum. Tension in one place can mean increased tension in another. The opposite is true as well: loss of tension in one place can mean loss of tension in the rest of the bondage. How tightly it is applied is an important structural part of the bondage scene. In general the appropriate amount is determined by whether the bondage can maintain structure under different moving conditions. This could be wiggling, changing poses, or actively trying to escape. Check in with the Bottom to see if something applied might end up being too tight as the material used in this bondage style has no stretch.

It is difficult to put chain on a body too tightly given the relative inflexibility of steel. When applying the bondage be sure that the tension is good enough to sustain its own position on the body as long as there is not extra slack pulling on the chain to loosen it. Any additional chain left over will work against you, so you may need to support it to prevent gravity being your enemy.

When you build single columns consider different attachments you are making. If you are creating one between a thigh and a chest, not only do you have the tension on the chain around each column, but you also have the tension of one wrap pulling on the other.

The more connections that are made the more tension may be increased, and soon bondage could become very uncomfortable and--from our perspective--unsustainable. Your scenes may end early, and what is the fun in that?

Experience

We are of the mind that unless it is intended to be *uncomfortable or painful on purpose* bondage shouldn't be something you have to "suffer through." It might be something to endure. It might be something to relish. It could be something to savor and to experience. It should never be something you do begrudgingly because of poor execution and sustainability.

We believe bondage should be a prolonged, shared experience. Whatever bondage brings you as a Top or as a Bottom you should have the opportunity to thrive being in it however that manifests itself. Sadistic bondage is a thing that exists, but also so does sensual bondage, as does bondage for sex. We don't think bondage has to be punishing though that can be the objective. That kind of thing falls under power dynamics which is a different matter altogether and has been written about at great length elsewhere.

Segmentation

As previously mentioned, we have about 100 feet of chain in our collection of hardware. This is not one continuous 100-foot strand. That would be impossible to work with and we don't even want to consider how to make anything happen with such an unwieldy length. Instead, our kit is broken down to segments that we know from experience would create wraps around different body parts.

Cecilia has a thigh measurement that is somewhere between 20 and 28 inches in circumference when relaxed, depending on the position to be bound in. In order to put chain bondage around her upper thigh a four foot piece of chain, or 48 inches, may not be sufficient depending on the way the leg is flexed and positioned while the single column is being placed. A five foot piece of chain, or 60 inches, works great with some left over to do something else with. An eight foot piece of chain might be wasteful as it could be used somewhere else to cover more parts of the body combined together.

Is having a bunch of five foot pieces of chain sufficient to cover every part of the body twice around? It depends on the Bottom. Do you ever intend to do chain bondage on anyone else? Would it be sufficient to use up your budget on connecting strands of chain together to perform double wraps where necessary? It could end up being very wasteful, and shorting your budget unnecessarily. This is where the idea of what you have in your budget meets the average clothing sizes of human beings, not the "ideal" size. There are also ways to use different lengths that fit the Bottom to your advantage, as shown on the model to the left.

Similar designs on the left and right thighs were created with different chain lengths. The design on the left leg is made from a single length of chain, and the design on the right is made of a few variable lengths. Functionally the designs create a repeating single column travelling down the leg, allowing for additional connections to be made. The design on the right leaves some leftover slack between sections that can be used creatively to attach to other potential locations of bondage on the body. The design to the left is arguably more aesthetic and complete. Both designs fit on the Bottom, with different intentional results.

The chain on the left thigh (as viewed) is one continuous eight-foot strand. The chain on the right is made up of multiple shorter sections.

In our experience, a great number of human beings have at least a 30 inch natural waist, with variation. A five foot piece of a chain (60 inches) might not make it fully twice around a lot of people. A six foot piece of chain (72 inches) could work well for more people, but if you want to be the kind of person who accommodates for all shapes and sizes of people (a.k.a. A Good Top) then it might be in your interest to own an eight foot (96 inches) chain segment as well for putting around a waist. If you own a 10 foot piece you can be increasingly assured that you can put a single column around the waist of a human being.

Proportion

There is an intense relationship between human beings and proportions and how those relate to bondage participants in alternative lifestyles. We are of the opinion that *anyone* can be in bondage despite the contrary pornographic representations of bondage Bottoms. A Good Top will have the capability to do so in their kit. Bondage is not the exclusive domain of those with the toxic marketed "ideal body type and size," whatever that means. Bondage is the domain of people *who want to be in bondage*.

The same applies to all of the other sizes in which a person might embody. Some people have very wide chests. Some people have narrow chests. Some of those people have wider hips. These are the things to consider as you build your kit to execute what it is that you'd like to do.

Slack

There are logistical considerations as well. These are the weight and manageability of longer lengths of chain. It doesn't make sense to use a 10 foot piece of chain where a six foot or five foot piece might suffice. Keeping tension becomes more difficult when you use sizes of chain that are inappropriate for the application at hand as the weight of the slack makes it more difficult to maneuver around a body part. For some people an extra length of chain whipping around could be unpleasant or dangerous depending on where it is happening.

Extra slack at an end can be useful but sometimes you want an aesthetic finish to a column where you've used the perfect size segment of chain such that there is almost none. This is the ideal scenario when creating bondage for photographs that also doesn't use any excess hardware to make it "neat". It reduces any visual noise of the bondage.

Having bondage with minimal slack also helps make complex designs relatively easier because there are less free ends to worry about managing or confusing with other free segments.

Choice

We covered the variety of connectors available for chain bondage usage in Chapter Three. When you're planning your chain bondage application, make a decision on the types of connectors you feel comfortable using in which places. Where does it make sense for you to use connectors that work in tension only? Do you want the flexibility of being able to attach anything at any place and not have to worry about detensioning before disassembly or escape?

Plan the assembly. Think about what should go where and why and in what orientation. Think about

how a connector will be able to come apart while in tension. Will you be able to get to the screw pin readily? Can it be undone later? Is this a primary connector that holds a lot of different tensioned wraps together? Does this attach more than one column? Does your Bottom need to get access to a limb or to get out right away? Having an answer to these questions as you build the bondage will start to affect the choices you make about chain bondage assembly as you become more proficient. This is not an all encompassing list but these are the kinds of questions you should consider when developing a plan.

Body

Where do you want to put the bondage? Did the Bottom give sober, informed, affirmative consent to receive bondage? What kind of shape do you want to put them in? Can they withstand it? Do they have injuries to avoid? Are you aware of nerves to avoid?

Many of these were discussed in Chapter Two and this might be a good time to review any responses and discussions you have had with your Bottom. You can never go wrong with asking for confirmation of something you have already negotiated upon.

There may be some instances of the bondage that are shown which might not be ideal for a particular person, and it is okay to consider modifying the structures to meet different needs. Modifying harnesses and patterns is a different challenge all by itself, so consider making sure that you have a good grasp on the basics of what is being shown before moving forward with any changes that might be necessary based on those needs.

Orientation

Something you might notice about chain is that it has the ability to roll and twist. Any length of chain can 'kink up', causing tension to be distributed unevenly when a wrap is placed on the body.

This kinking will make the chain harder to work with as it will sometimes fight to stay put as you're placing it on a body. If the chain is twisting it will resist you as you attempt to secure it together. Twisting also causes the chain to get shorter by incremental amounts. You can test this yourself by taking one end of your chain and twisting it repeatedly until it kinks up really badly. A bad kinking will be obvious because of the size of chain used but subtle kinking may not be.

Be sure that as you're placing a wrap on a body part you're getting all of the kinks and twists out. You will struggle far less if you manage the chain beforehand and also during the bondage. In general placing a connector to finish a wrap will usually 'fix' the position of the chain but if you fix a wrap before getting the kinks out, the Bottom may feel more pressure in the body part with the wrap on it.

A kinked chain makes it more difficult to close a wrap as well as it can cause the connector to rotate unfavorably on its own.

Hands

Up until now, just about every subjective part of chain bondage has been covered including preferences on chain, connectors, non-connectors, and practical thoughts on negotiation and consent. There is one more very important detail to share before we get into the examples which is the subject of hands and hand dexterity.

With any type of new skill there are subtleties of movement that must be learned that are not usually formally taught. Imagine the first time you ever learned how to use a tool: scissors, a screwdriver, a hammer, or a saw. Was the way to use them intuitive for you? Were you taught how to use your hands and arms to operate the tool most effectively?

With this particular style of bondage you may find that there are some challenges to doing a few things at once with your hands. For example, being able to hold two pieces together under tension while inserting and closing a connector, or inserting a screw pin. Learning how to do this for yourself will take a little bit of work to figure out what is the best way for you though there are some ways that might get you going in the right direction.

We generally use a technique for holding that we call "the claw".

"The Claw"

This technique uses the thumb, the index and middle fingers for holding things together without obstructing what needs to happen by folding in the last two fingers. The ring and pinky fingers are usually reserved for guiding and holding slack, or anything else that might need to be supported.

Chain bondage involves the idea of one hand holding and the other hand doing. The claw is a reasonable technique for keeping chain links in place while another operation has to be done with those links.

The benefit to using this hand position is that the holding between the thumb and index finger doesn't require a lot of conscious thought to use. The webbing (or 'thenar webspace') is a good place to squeeze things into position which will aid in holding half of the tension in a wrap. The other half of the tension in the chain is being maintained by the index and middle fingers.

Using the claw for the start of a split wrap single column.

While tension is being maintained by one hand, the other hand can do things like manipulate a chain link into a common link, attach a shackle or other connector, or close the connector by twisting a nut or a pin. By attaching a connector to the chain being held by the index and middle fingers, you create a larger grip on that side to hold tension making the chain link less likely to slip out of your fingers, depending on your grip strength and if the chain is wet or not.

Holding the chain with the left hand, and manipulating the common link with the right.

Holding the chain with the common link held into position and ready to be used.

One hand holding, the other hand getting ready to attach the shackle.

After the shackle is in place, the hand holding will have a bigger gripping area on the right.

Tension is being maintained while the other hand operates the pin of the shackle.

The same claw technique used on the single-end wrap, a different style single column.

This technique is also good for manipulating connectors that might already be attached but need to be rotated in order to keep tension, or to put them into their correct final position. As mentioned previously anchor shackles need to be used in an in-line way to be the most effective and to not reduce their WLL.

This shackle is already in a position, but needs to be attached in an in-line fashion.

One hand is holding the common link and tension, and the other is holding and manipulating the shackle.

The claw is being used to hold the shackle and common link in place so that the pin can be secured.

One hand is holding the shackle and common link, and the other hand is operating the pin.

Even though there are situations where the claw is useful this is not the only way to perform the claw, nor is it the only way to manage tension or to hold connectors while performing chain bondage. Here are a few other variations that might work for you. Ultimately it is up to you to figure out what approach works best. You may find one that is vastly better than ours and as long as it works for you, absolutely use it!

A slight variation of the claw where the chain is being tensioned off of the thumb, rather than the common link being held between the thumb and hand.

An overhand grip where the middle and ring fingers are positioned to hold the bow of the shackle down while the thumb and index finger are holding the common link into position for pin placement.

There are some instances where you might be tempted to put a finger through some of the chain links and in general this does work okay. It does come with a minor warning: be careful which fingers you put through the chain links and how much tension that the finger is holding.

The human fingers are very strong in a folding, grasping way. They are also very good at pinching and squeezing, but they are slightly less stable at side to side movement. It is possible to have a finger injury holding the chain in this way but as long as you are careful it should be less of an issue. Specifically, there is a risk of finger dislocation that can happen that you should be aware of.

The thumb is placed inside of the two chain links that are right before the common link with the index and middle fingers holding the shackle into position.

Your First Single Column - The Thigh Cuff

There are two basic ways to do a single column. Whichever style you prefer is up to you, but there are advantages to doing either. The concept shown here is the application of a single column around a point on the thigh, but it can be applied to other areas of the body as well. If you're unsure about chain sizes to use recall the thought from "Considerations" to think about sizes of clothing.

Single-End Wrap (Thigh Cuff I)

The advantage to the single-end wrap is that it allows you to choose where the slack will end up if you have any left afterwards. This slack can be useful when connecting to other places, such as body parts like the waist or the chest. The single-end wrap only requires one connector to complete, but it is a little bit more difficult because there is more holding that needs to happen during its placement. Place the thigh cuff at the thickest part of the leg for the best tension.

Step 1:

Pick a point on the outside of the thigh that is in-line with the hip bone.

Step 2:

Wrap a length of chain around in either direction and prepare to connect the end to the common link.

Make sure that the length of chain you choose can travel at least twice around the thigh.

Step 3:

When attaching the shackle be sure to orient it in such a way that the bow of the shackle is attached to the free end, the pin threads are facing towards the Bottom, and the common link will eventually be attached to the shackle using the pin.

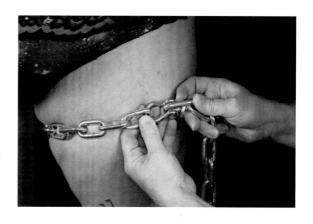

Step 4:

Temporarily side-load the shackle and reverse tension the wrap starting at the common link. This will determine the direction that the single column wraps, either up or down the thigh. Make sure that the shackle has the threaded side on the right to ensure correct pin orientation later on.

It is critical that this initial wrap is fairly tight, but not so tight that it is uncomfortable.

Step 5:

Send the remaining slack around the thigh and prepare to finish the reverse tensioned wrap by picking a new common link to attach to the side loaded shackle.

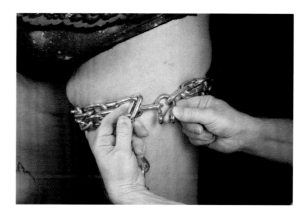

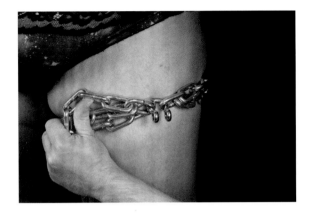

Step 6:

Attach the second common link in the following orientation (as shown) to the side-loaded shackle. The second common link should be on the open side of the shackle. Pay attention to the direction of the slack. Again, make sure that this wrap is also sufficiently tight.

Step 7:

Holding the shackle and the initial common link, re-orient the shackle to an in-line position with that link ready to receive the pin. Make sure to have a good grip on the links so you don't lose them in transition.

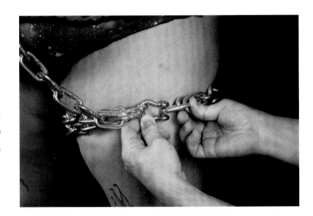

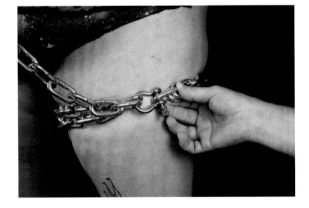

Step 8:

Insert pin through shackle and initial common link to complete the cuff. The orientation of the cuff will reflect the direction chosen in **Step 4**.

Note:

Manage any remaining slack to avoid it becoming an obstacle to further bondage or attach elsewhere (or hold it up to take a good photo!)

Split-Wrap (Thigh Cuff II)

The split-wrap cuff is a little less complex to construct, but requires at least two connectors to complete. The basic premise of this single column is that you are performing two reverse tensions--one on each side of the connector--and making sure to create two common links. There is not as much holding required as the tension in both the first and second wraps do a pretty good job of keeping the column in place.

A minor disadvantage is that there will be a little more of a challenge in terms of placement and the direction of available extra slack to work with. Instead of just a single trailing segment that you can dictate the orientation of, there are two shorter ends that have only the choice of going up or down (or outwards). An advantage is that this single column does not require the manipulation of a connector that has already been placed.

Step 1:

Wrap a length of chain sufficiently long enough to travel twice around the thigh, making the slack equal length from the meeting point. In this case we started at the front and are making the first connection in the back of the thigh.

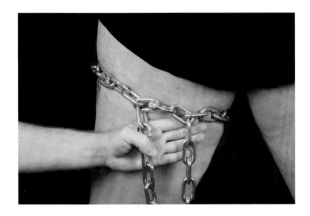

Step 2:

Attach the two slack segments together with a shackle creating two common links and being sure to direct the remaining trails in the opposite directions. The open side of the shackle should be facing you when placing it.

Step 3:

Return the slack ends around the front and prepare to attach the segments together by creating another set of common links to manage any remaining slack.

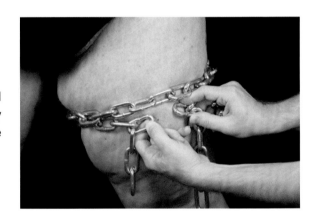

Step 4:

Attach the common links together with an in-line shackle with the open side facing you again and complete the single column!

Links for Success

Now that you have been shown how to create the basic single columns that will be used throughout this book, here are some helpful tips that might be useful to you. Some of these are tips to avoid bad form or because the kinds of handling operations are perhaps not intuitive. Others are here because of skipped steps or poor orientation. Others yet are accidental, but hopefully this section will help you avoid these common errors and reduce any struggling you might have in your bondage technique.

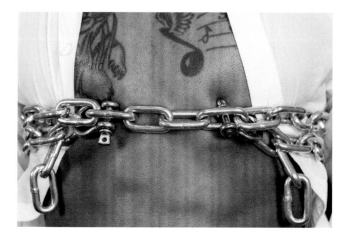

Flipped Shackle

No matter which single column you perform, it is critical to the Bottom to be sure that the shackle is facing the correct direction. Having the pin face towards the Bottom can cause discomfort at a minimum to extreme pain at a maximum depending on the tension and location of the bondage. Always be sure to have the pins facing outwards when using shackles as in the shackle to the right in this example of a split-wrap column placed on a chest.

Side-loaded Shackle

In Chapter Three the anchor shackle was introduced as the premier connector to use in chain bondage. Part of using an anchor shackle in the Single-End wrap involved temporarily side-loading the shackle in step 4. While it is appropriate to sometimes side-load the shackle as a part of a step always be sure to correct the loading of the shackle to an in-line fashion in the proper orientation before moving onto other parts of the bondage. Doing so will keep your

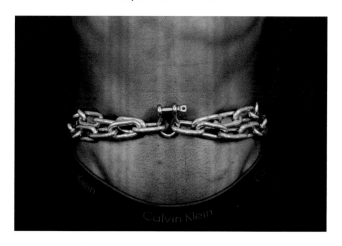

shackles from accidentally deforming due to loading them in this configuration.

Temporarily side-loading a shackle can also be useful if you're trying to hold the position and tension of chain on a body while completing a connector manipulation, such as in this example of the Single-End wrap column where a side-loaded shackle is holding tension until it can be put into the correct in-line orientation. The slack that would normally be pulling the single column down towards the floor is being directed upwards toward a waist line. This way, there is less concern about trying to hold the

position of the single column while good tension is still maintained. One of the last things you want to have happen while you're performing bondage (especially on someone standing) is for gravity to have part in pulling a single column down the leg of your Bottom, and performing this helpful measure will reduce struggling and having a fear of needing more than two hands.

This will be particularly useful in the first harness, 'The Gunslinger', shown in Chapter Five.

This technique can also be helpful if your tension is less than perfect, or because there might be a lot of humidity, or due to the shape of the Bottom's thighs.

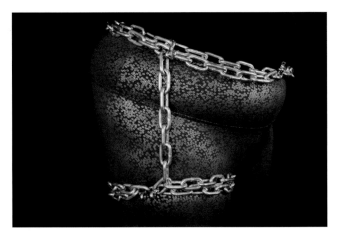

The end goal of this is to reduce the amount of holding that has to occur when orientation of a shackle has to change. Forgetting to modify the shackle afterwards and leaving it in a side-loaded state has a detrimental effect on the tension of a single column whether it be the Single-End wrap or the Split-Wrap.

Using a side-loaded shackle in a long term way is not only not good for the connector, but it also changes the position of the slack or reverse tension. Normally when good tension is made, there should not be very much room in the single column to slide one or more fingers underneath the wraps. Because the shape of the bow of the anchor shackle is round it does not hold a side-loaded position indefinitely. The distance between the opposite sides of the bow is shorter than the distance between

the bow and where the pin connection is made. This means that when the shackle shifts there is a lengthening that occurs and tension is lost potentially causing the single column to slide down the thigh on one side and eventually having it fall apart entirely while still attached.

If other bondage is attached to the single-column the potential for that bondage to come out of position is increased as well.

Learning to reorient shackles that are in place is one of the more important skills to learn in chain bondage. Not only will it help you keep your bondage together, but it can also help you readjust the sizing of single or double columns if it ever becomes necessary in a more dynamic situation.

It will also become extremely important when mastering the choice and orientation of the common link to direct reverse tensions and slack appropriately.

Anchoring the Free End

When creating the Single-End wrap column, placing a shackle or other connector on the end you hold as a secondary step may not be an ideal way for you to put a single column together. It might benefit you to have some planning done in advance to assist in the assembly of the column.

Preemptively placing the anchor shackle on the free end of the chain is an excellent way to provide a grip to maintain control of the chain. Attach the anchor shackle so that the bow is through the end link, and then place the chain link between the fingers you will use to hold that end as shown.

It's not absolutely necessary to use your thumb and index finger to hold the shackle: it is up to you what feels comfortable.

Placing the shackle at the end as a primary step does mean that you have to pay a little bit more attention to the orientation of the shackle before the rest of the column can be completed. Be sure that the threaded part of the shackle is facing the Bottom, with the pin handle side facing you and that you intend to wrap the reverse tension going upwards (assuming that you're placing it on the thigh of a person standing and that is the direction you are intending to travel.) If the Bottom's thigh is in a different orientation, make sure that the shackle is still in this position. It is always the case that for the Single-End Wrap that the bow side of the shackle is attached to two chain links and the pin side is attached to one.

Extreme Asymmetry

In general you should avoid placing highly asymmetrical split-wrap columns. Aside from being aesthetically poor it can also cause problems with unintentional overlap. Creating these asymmetrical single columns can cause issues while trying to apply even tension as well. Some of the harnesses shown later rely on having equal lengths around the body in various places, and being able to control this problem early on will be a benefit to you.

Self-crossing Chain

When placing single columns make sure that the chain does not cross over itself as you secure the single columns. While this cuff in this example appears to be tensioned correctly, it is definitely not, and the way it has been placed around the leg can cause the whole thigh cuff to roll over itself in one direction or another depending on body orientation and gravity. Thigh cuffs like these will not hold and may cause pain for the Bottom wearing them as there will be a pressure point at the place where the chain crosses over itself.

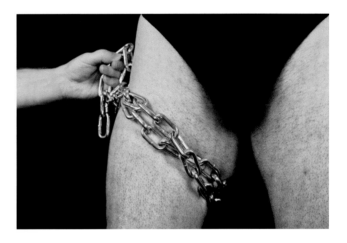

Uneven Tension - Poor Tension

Proper tension is extremely important to have in bondage whether you're the Top placing it or the Bottom wearing it. As shown in the example poor tension can also be uneven tension from one side to the other. In this split-wrap around a waist the reverse tension on the right side of the split-wrap is much tighter than the reverse tension around the left. This can cause a number of issues: discomfort, pain, poor fit and wearability of the bondage, or poor structure in combining different bondage elements together. Not to mention that uneven tension can also cause extreme asymmetry which can further cause difficulties in the rest of the bondage. Uneven tension can also cause problems in releasing the Bottom out of the bondage on their body in the event of an emergency. When you're placing the split-wrap single column, be sure to apply the same amounts of tension on both sides.

Poor tension can also result in two wraps not being aligned next to each other in a single column. You want to be sure that all of your wraps are neat and evenly tensioned regardless of how you perform them. It is difficult to put chain on *too tightly*. You want to put the wraps on so they're just tight enough to help hold their own position, but not so tight that they're causing pain or discomfort to the Bottom.

Uneven tension doesn't just apply to the split-wrap single column. It is possible when placing the Single-End Wrap to place uneven tension on the upper and lower lines around the thigh. Poor tension will cause the single column to fall right off no matter how high on the thigh it is placed. The Single-End Wrap relies on both parts around the thigh to be tensioned evenly to maintain position and connectability to other parts of the overall bondage.

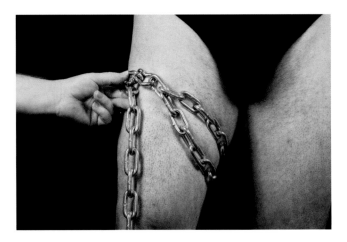

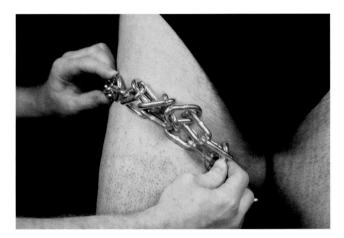

Twisted Chain Links

It is possible while placing the bondage, that twists exist in the links. Twisted chain links can be a problem because they cause the chain to be shortened and tensioned in a very unfavorable way. An extreme and exaggerated twist is shown in the example to the left: six chain links are kinked up together that take up the length of three links below it.

Having twists in your chain can cause the subsequent links to be directed somewhat unpredictably, so be sure to untwist your chain if you're having problems with rolling or other manipulation that should be "correct". Signs could include having difficulty putting a connector in the right orientation, "fighting" the chain to hold it into place, finding that chain on one side of the body does not connect in the same way as on the other despite equal length ends, or having trouble maintaining tension. This list is not fully exhaustive because even with just one twist the effects can be subtle but still troublesome.

One way to avoid this is to not use excessive amounts of chain for a particular single column. The excess pulls down on the bondage while you're working with it requiring you to fight with the orientation of the chain at the same time. There are ways to mitigate this but even if you are able to prevent the slack from pulling down while you're placing it, dealing with the directionality of the slack can be somewhat unmanageable.

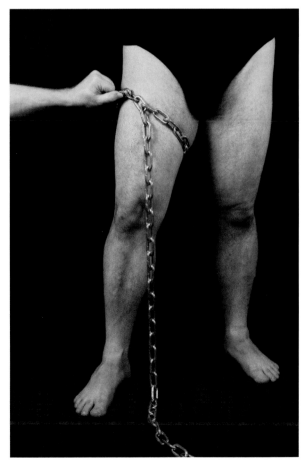

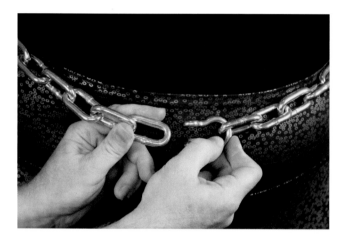

Chain Isn't Long Enough

Sometimes you may run into the opposite problem: having a length of chain that isn't long enough. It may be that you are towards the end of your current budget and need to place an additional part of bondage.

In this example the length of the chain is about half as long as necessary to place a Split-Wrap single column around the waist.

If you have a piece of chain that is not long enough to do what you like, then you can attach another piece. It is okay to do so as long as you have it in your kit.

Whichever connector that you use to attach an additional length, make sure that it is placed in an orientation where you have the closing hardware accessible or facing you whether that be the nut on the quick link or the pin of the shackle.

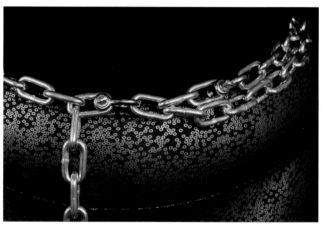

The additional length can be added anywhere with any connector and then used as a single length of chain. The best method is to connect the ends of the two lengths of chain together so that it forms a continuous line. If you're extending a length to make a Split-Wrap (for this example), remember to leave extra slack hanging down from the original chain length to make the single column correctly.

If you were adding an additional length of chain to form the Single-End Wrap single column, then be mindful of the position of the connector that is used to attach the two lengths together. If you can, try to avoid having it near the location where the primary shackle would go when the slack is redirected.

Poor Common Link Positioning

There are ways to use the common link that are "technically correct" but might cause functional issues. One of these is positioning the common link in such a way that it is a pivot.

Placing a shackle in the middle of the common link with the bow of the shackle as a pivot allows for a lot of rotation on that link, depending on the tension applied on the initial wrap or in the reverse tension.

Additionally, this will cause the two wraps to have a gap and not keep their structure. As in the photo, the reverse tension is starting to trail off in a direction that is not parallel to the initial tensioned wrap.

Similar problems can happen if the pin of the shackle is placed in the middle of the common link. Though the two wraps may be traveling in the same direction the space between them is definitely much larger and there can be a shift in tension that changes the alignment of all of the chain links in this orientation.

It is easy to place the common link in a poor position, and cause the bondage to have loose tension. It can be damaging to the Bottom, aesthetically poor, and make applications of techniques listed further in this book difficult--especially those that rely on good tension.

Cuffs Too Tight

When you're placing a non-chain cuff on a person make sure it is not on too tightly (or too loosely.) Putting cuffs on too tightly can cause blood chokes which may mask nerve impingements. It also reduces the amount of time the Bottom can be in the scene due to pain from the tightness and loss of feeling.

Blood chokes can cause the restricted area to swell with one of the worst case scenarios being a clot and a visit to the emergency room, or lesser worse case being severe nerve damage.

A consequence of putting on a cuff too tightly is that it makes the cuff hard to remove. It is usually difficult to put on a cuff too tight but depending on the way it was manufactured, extra strength may not be required to do so. This is an instance of the importance of knowing the way that your equipment operates. Always check in with the Bottom to make sure that the cuffs are reasonably tight and not restrictive in a negative way.

It is more likely that you can get the cuffs on too tightly when the hand is relaxed. If the Bottom is either splaying their fingers or making a fist there will be some room underneath the cuff when they relax their hand. It may be the case that it is better for the Bottom to tense their hand and wrist before the cuff goes on but this is not a universal recommendation.

Some indications that a cuff is on too tightly may be discoloration, swelling of the veins on the back of the hand, loss of feeling, pain, loss of flexural movement at the wrist, or lack of grip strength. There may be other symptoms that are not included in this list.

Lack of Scene Sustainability

There are some bondage harnesses and poses that are more sustainable than others over a longer period of time. It is better to perform those bondage elements first because the Bottom has limited time and endurance available in the scene once it gets going. Because the Arms Behind Chest Harness is less sustainable for most people, doing it first may not be the best course of action because that is now your limiting factor of the length of the scene.

In this instance a lower body harness may have been a better starting point because the end result was a hogtie pose. The hogtie pose is a face-down chest-down bondage position that can restrict breathing and cause discomfort for the Bottom once it has been completed. Because the chest harness was the first part of the hogtie executed, there was not time to perform a lower body bondage harness.

Chapter 5 - Harnesses

The Gunslinger Hip Harness

This hip harness is a combination of the first single column that was shown as Thigh Cuff I and a single column around the (natural) waist as a slight variation of Thigh Cuff II. It is a harness that allows thigh cuffs to be anchored to a line around the waist to maintain their position while providing attachment points on the thighs to extend bondage possibilities.

The gunslinger is an example of how single columns can be used to build a basic harness which is a core concept of chain bondage. There are later examples that illustrate how the power of single column combinations can be harnessed so be sure you have a good handle on being able to construct the Thigh Cuff I single column as it can be a little tricky to master. Your ability to manage direction of the slack through the positioning of the common link will be critical going forward.

Creating this harness is also a good test of your ability to make wraps and single columns sufficiently tight to be useful and will help you develop the muscle memory required for future harnesses.

Step 1:

Begin by forming the start of the split-wrap single column around the waist connecting in an inline fashion. Note the rotation of the common links on either side of the shackle. The open side of the shackle should be facing you.

Step 2:

Reverse tension the slack and secure to the existing single wrap. It is not critical for the slack to meet up in the middle as long as you are travelling some distance back around the waist.

It is okay to use additional shackles if you started with a shorter length of chain.

Step 3:

Build the single-end wrap thigh cuff upwards and attach the slack to the single column around the waist. You can keep the thigh cuff temporarily incomplete to make it easier to finish by avoiding the gravitational pull of the remaining slack while you anchor it to the waistline (see **Step 6** of Thigh Cuff I, or "Side-Loaded Shackle" under "Links for Success".)

Step 4:

Attach the slack to the waist by using a shackle and creating the common link so any remaining slack pulls down.

Step 5:

Complete the thigh cuff if you left it unfinished and locate a position on the thigh cuff to attach any leftover slack with a shackle.

Step 6:

Attach any leftover slack to the thigh cuff. It doesn't have to look exactly as shown here, but try to make it look pleasing and unobstructive.

Step 7:

Repeat **Step 3** through **Step 6** on the other thigh and complete the hip harness!

The Mermaid (Legs Together) Hip Harness

Any harness that binds the legs together without the bondage traveling in-between them is referred to as a 'Mermaid Harness', for obvious reasons.

This harness is both decorative and functional. It is also extendable if it is built on a repeating unit.

How much movement your bottom has relies on the amount of tension you put around the legs. The more tension the more inflexible and stiff they are. Too loose and you might let the Bottom wiggle away undesirably.

This particular harness can be budget-heavy. You can build this harness by using much longer lengths and adapting the design or you can use much shorter segments with more connectors and save your longer lengths for other intentions.

Keep in mind that this harness creates a possible falling risk. If you engage in power-play situations that restrict how the Bottom moves, be aware of the potential danger and use appropriate measures to avoid a gnarly incident.

Step 1:

Create a split-wrap single column around the natural waist or hips (whichever is more comfortable) with the split point at the center in the front.

Step 2:

On the outsides of both thighs hang equal lengths of chain such that they dangle down and bisect the thigh as evenly as possible. You may have to reposition this in order to make further attachments more equal.

The lengths that you hang will determine the overall length of this harness. It can be shorter or longer relative to your preference.

Step 3:

In the front and the back hang lengths of chain that are twice as long as the ones hanging on the outsides of the thighs, but are doubled up so they end up being the same length (or slightly longer).

Note:

Make the attachments in the front and the back in this triangular fashion creating common links on either side of the center whether that is the shackle, or the center link.

Step 4:

On one side of the thighs attach two links together from the dangling front and back lengths of chain on that side, some distance down from the waist or hip column. Make sure that they end up being as close to the same length as possible. Attach them together using a shackle that travels through a link that reduces the amount of sagging slack to a minimum, but is not fully tensioned. The goal is to create a six-pointed asterisk.

Note:

The six-pointed asterisk should have common links on the pin and bow of the shackle that redirect the slack to point back down towards the centerline between the legs. Be sure that the shackle that creates this design is loaded in an in-line fashion with the pin facing outwards.

Step 5:

Repeat **Step 4** on the other side of the body. Then attach the front and back sets of slack together with shackles that create additional common links to establish the pattern. At this point you should have a tensioned diamond on the front and back. The chain that falls down the outsides of the legs will still have some looseness to it and should still travel straight down--it is mostly there to help organize the rest of the harness.

Note:

Make sure to attach the bottom of the diamond on the front and back together leaving a common link to attach more slack, if necessary.

Step 6:

To continue the diamond pattern attach additional lengths of chain if necessary, and repeat **Step 4** and **Step 5** further down the outsides of the thighs. Make sure to have free-end common links to direct the chain. Be aware of the pressure the second diamond will be putting on the outsides and caps of the knees.

Note:

Try to start the bottom of the first diamond / top of the second diamond at a favorable position. The sides of the second diamond (the second asterisks) on the thighs should sit above the kneecaps. In the image the point above the kneecaps ends at the same place as the shorts.

Step 7:

Either end here to complete the harness, or continue to make a third diamond, or add cuffs and do more as you see fit.

Note:

If you choose to add ankle cuffs, be sure to tension the line that travels down the outsides of the thighs, adding lengths of chain if necessary. This will improve the overall tension and shape of the harness.

Note:

When the harness is complete, the Bottom will only be able to move in very tiny ways. This is the riskiest for falls because it is the most restrictive.

The Folded Leg Harness

The folded leg is one of the harnesses that is both useful to learn and versatile. Being able to capture the leg in a folded position is actually more enabling of different bondage poses because it is often easier for the Bottom to have their leg this way while in positions that might require certain forced leg orientations, with the exception of those Bottoms that have knee and leg joint mobility issues.

A downside is that there are a lot of steps to complete it with possibilities for variation in the application of the chain depending on technique and body. The general objective is to position the ankle and calf as close as possible against the back of the thigh, but the distance from the ankle to the front side of the thigh will be different for everybody.

The distance between the cuff and the place just below the kneecap will also vary greatly. The approach we use is the most basic version of a way to accomplish this harness while still maintaining the awareness of bodily proportions and lengths of chains required without having an excess of slack that can't be put to use. It also minorly improvises on the existing ideas of the thigh cuffs that have already been demonstrated.

Step 1:

Begin by attaching an ankle cuff to the shin, slightly above the ankle and resting at the base of the calf muscle.

Step 2:

Attach a length of chain to the ankle cuff on the side that is facing the inner thigh. Be sure that the length of the chain is enough to wrap twice around a thigh with a bit of slack left over.

Step 3:

Wrap around the thigh going outside to the ankle and as close to the groin as possible. Generally the closer this is, the better it will stay on. Be sure to check in with the Bottom if this is an acceptable place to put bondage on their body.

Step 4:

Continue the wrap around the thigh going in between the thigh and the calf and wrapping upwards towards the knee, ending at the other cuff attachment point on the outside of the thigh.

Step 5:

Attach the slack to the ankle cuff on the side facing out, creating a common link to direct the slack upwards.

Note:

Pay close attention to the way the common link attaches to the ankle cuff using a shackle. Placing the shackle in this orientation (bow at the cuff) reduces shifting of the tension to a minimum.

Step 6:

Attach a shackle to secure the upper and lower band of the thigh cuff together on the outside where the wrap around the thigh meets the slack that attaches to the ankle cuff.

Step 7:

Repeat the shackle attachment on the inside of the thigh.

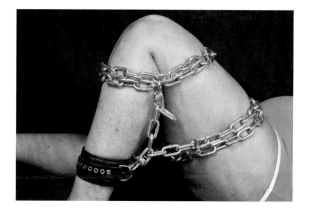

Step 8:

Create a split-wrap cuff at the top of the folded leg about two to three fingers below the bottom of the kneecap, where there may be a softer, flatter spot right above the place where the shin bone starts to be obvious. If you create this cuff with the middle shackle oriented between the crease and the middle of the upper thigh, you may have extra slack left over on the inner side of the thigh that can be used in the next few steps.

Step 9:

Attach the slack from **Step 5** to the upper cuff with a shackle creating a common link to direct any remaining slack downwards. If the person you're putting bondage on is able to close their leg very tightly then you may have more slack left over after this step. **If this is the case, then consider the Alternative Steps at the end of this series.**

83

Step 10:

Attach the remaining slack to the lower wrap using more than one shackle if needed.

Note:

Pay attention to the orientation of the shackles to make sure that the pins aren't facing inwards against the Bottom's leg.

Step 11:

Attach the slack left over on the inside of the leg from **Step 8** down to the shackle that was attached at **Step 7**. If there is no slack left over then use a series of connectors. That will complete the harness!

Alternative Step 9:

If the Bottom is able to get their calf very close to their thigh, then use the remaining slack to attach to the upper double wrap, and then back down towards the ankle.

Be sure to create a common link off of the attached connector on the upper split-wrap cuff.

Alternative Step 10:

Attach the final slack on the outside of the leg to the ankle cuff. If you have extra slack left over, you can either manage it, or attach it to another location to extend the bondage position.

Alternative Step 11:

Attach a shorter piece of chain to the shackle placed on the inside of the thigh from **Step 7**.

Alternative Step 12:

Direct the length of chain up towards the split-wrap cuff placed around the folded leg from **Step 9**.

Alternative Step 13:

Attach the slack to the upper cuff with a shackle and direct it back down towards the ankle with a common link.

Alternative Step 14:

Complete the folded leg by connecting the slack to the inside ring of the ankle cuff with a shackle.

The Crossed Legs Harness

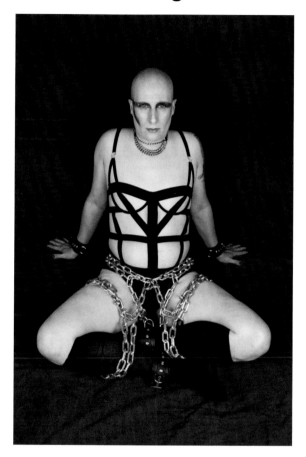

What's better than one folded leg? Two folded legs! The Crossed Legs Harness allows the Bottom to sit in the well-known "criss-cross-apple-sauce" pose that we all learned in childhood. Rather than starting at the ankles like the Folded Leg Harness, the Crossed Legs harness begins at the waist and gathers each leg close to the pelvis, and tucks the feet in near the groin.

A Bottom bound in this harness will feel restrained and dependent on their Top as they cannot get up to walk or easily crawl away.

Posture matters in this position. The Bottom should be sitting up on the base of their pelvis with a straightened spine. With some people the better the posture the closer the legs can be folded inwards. This position can be made more comfortable by having the bottom sit with their Sitz bones on a cushion or bolster.

This harness is demonstrated with one column on each leg but the pattern can be repeated along the folded leg based on the shape of the Bottom's legs and how closely they can tuck their feet in.

Step 1:

Attach ankle cuffs to the Bottom and have them sit in a cross-legged fashion.

Step 2:

Create a split-wrap single column around the waist, with the remaining slack directed towards the front. Choose a length of chain that is longer than twice around the Bottom's waist.

Note:

When directing the slack from the front be sure to connect the trailing ends two empty links away from each other in the center of the split-wrap column with shackles. Orient the slack towards the ankle cuffs.

Step 3:

Attach the first slack to the ankle cuff that is further away from the groin. The slack will travel under the opposite calf and over the top of the ankle. You may have to get the Bottom to lift the other leg that is closer to their own body so that you can make the connection.

Step 4:

Make the connection with the second slack to the ankle cuff that is closest to their groin. There may be remaining slack left over that is not utilized for the rest of the harness.

It is okay to tuck it away or let it lie.

Step 5:

Attach a new length of chain to one of the empty links in the center on the waistline and direct it around the front of the closest shin and under the thigh of that same leg.

Note:

Continue wrapping until you travel twice around that folded leg.

The length of the chain should be long enough to make a second wrap around that same thigh and shin, with the end of that length reaching at least the crease between the upper and lower leg.

Step 6:

Secure that folded leg by attaching the second wrap to the first at approximately one to two links above the crease between the calf and the inner thigh. There may be slack remaining that can be tucked in between the leg crease, or used later.

Join the chain that you used to make the single column around the shin and thigh at a point below the previous shackle used to secure the two wraps together.

Note:

The location and distance between the two shackles on this folded leg column are important to the execution of the harness.

The placements will affect an optional step to attach a second folded leg single column that sits closer to the knee (not pictured, but you can use a single-end thigh cuff for this application and attach it to the slack in the first part of **Step 6**.)

Step 7:

Repeat **Step 5** and **Step 6** on the other leg to complete the harness! If you perform the optional step of a single-end thigh cuff for one side, repeat it for the other.

Arms-Free Chest Harnesses

A chest harness is a pretty versatile bondage technique. There are lots of ways to adapt it for your use as well as providing many attachment points for other places on the body where bondage might exist. There are a few variations on an arms-free chest harness that you can do using existing single column techniques. Here are three shown that feature different pieces of hardware that might make it more flexible for whatever the situation demands. All of these provide comfort for the Bottom, but could be adapted for sadistic purposes.

One thing to note about chest harnesses is that not all people have the same amount of breast tissue to replicate the harnesses exactly. There may be adjustments required due to different sizing, because of surgical scarring that needs to be avoided, possible triggers, or because of either hypersensitivity or a lack of sensitivity. In such cases and depending on the negotiation, it is potentially better to place the bottom column just below the nipple, or to consider changing direction of the bottom column to travel around the smallest part of the waist.

If that is the desired option then make sure to avoid crossing over the floating ribs and accommodate for the larger gap between the bottom column and the top column. Note that this modification does come with a possible change in breathing for the Bottom which may or may not be a negotiated predicament.

If neither of these options are sufficient then consider against using the bottom column altogether. There are plenty of attachment points available on the top column for other bondage to attach to.

Arms Free Variant I

This variant is assembled only with shackles. This makes it a great harness to work with that doesn't require extra hardware. The only disadvantage is that putting together all of the connections in the back can be a little less straightforward and busy looking, but it does still have a clean functionality and is organized.

If the Bottom has a longer torso or you choose to go with the aforementioned modification on the previous page, additional shackles or connectors can be used in the back to keep the lower column supported. Choosing to use any remaining slack from the top column to support the bottom column will pull down on the lower wrap of the top column only, which can cause tension issues or discomfort in the harness.

Step 1:

Place a split-wrap single column above the breast/pectoral muscles so the common links and shackle are over the top of the sternum. The split-point should be in the front.

It isn't necessary to have the split-wrap column meet together in the back.

Step 2:

Place a split-wrap single column below the breast/pectoral muscles so the common links and shackle are over the sternum. This double wrap should be above the floating ribs.

Note: if you don't have lengths that are long enough to continuously wrap twice around the Bottom, then it is okay to combine segments together using shackles to complete this step.

Step 3:

In order to keep the bottom column from traveling downwards, attach it to the top column using two or more shackles on the back in a vertical fashion depending on the length of the Bottom's torso. Make sure not to side load any shackles. The horizontal distance between the vertical shackles should be minimized to prevent poor shape of the top and bottom columns.

Step 4:

After making the rear connections the harness is complete!

You can elect to dress the slack if you so choose.

Arms Free Variant II - Triangle Ring

The triangle ring version starts the same way as variant I but changes the way the back connections are made to reduce clutter with multiple shackles. See "Non-Connector Links" under Chapter Three to reference the particular hardware used in this variant. Pay close attention when acquiring hardware for this use to make sure that the triangle ring and chain size that you use both fit over the pin of the shackle, meaning that the triangle wire size should be just barely smaller than the chain wire size.

This variant may be a little tricky to execute due to the possibility that the lower wraps have more slack leftover and because the triangle ring adds some additional length on the bottom wrap, you may not have any choice in the length of the chain you use for those wraps. In this case the benefit of using less hardware with better organization means that less connectors are used in the harness.

Step 1:

Place a split-wrap single column above the breast/pectoral muscles so the common links and shackle are over the top of the sternum. The split-point should be in the front.

Step 2:

Attach the triangle ring over the pin of the shackle such that it sits adjacent to the chain link the pin is connected to.

Note:

The triangle and the chain used should both be able to fit over the pin in between the ends of the shackle. The pin should be resting close to or over the spine to keep the harness centered.

Step 3:

Find the centers of two lengths of chain that when doubled over will wrap around each side of the Bottom. These two lengths will have common links joined together with a shackle in the front.

Connect those lengths together and wrap both of them around the Bottom making sure that the pin of the shackle is facing outwards away from their body.

Step 4:

Place a shackle towards the ends of each wrap so that the bow of the shackle travels through two adjacent links. The placement of the shackle should be just far enough away from the ends to make a tensioned connection to the triangle with the pin side.

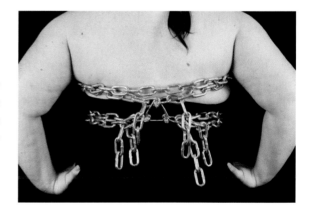

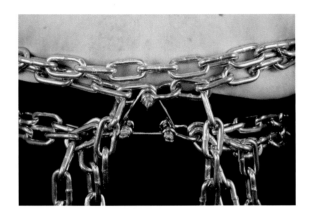

Step 5:

Pivot the triangle as needed about the top pin in order to make a tight connection on the lower wraps.

Make sure that the links that the shackles are attached to are treated like common links to maintain directionality of any leftover slack.

Arms Free Variant III - O-Ring

The O-Ring variant of this harness is the least complex of the three. The ring organizes all of the attaching shackles and creates a very aesthetic look on the chest. The result curves well to conform to some body types, but uses the cylinder-to-cylinder shackle orientation in making the connections on the back. The ring on the front allows for better access when making positional modifications to the way the wraps sit on the chest.

Step 1:

Attach the bow of a shackle onto the two free ends of a length of chain and attach the pin of the shackle onto the O-ring. Perform this on both sides of the O-ring.

Make sure the ring sits over the top of the sternum.

Step 2:

Attach the two lengths together in the back using the cylinder-to-cylinder shackle connection style (as shown in Chapter 3.)

Use common links to orient any slack left from the single column. Make sure the shackle that is in a horizontal orientation has the pin facing away from the Bottom.

Step 3:

Attach two additional lengths to the ring in the same fashion as in **Step 1**.

Adjust the ring slightly down towards the middle of the chest and wrap the new doubled-over lengths below the breasts/pectoral muscles and around to the back.

Step 4:

Repeat **Step 2** for the lower set of wraps, connecting the shackles in the same fashion.

Arms-Behind Chest Harness

The Arms-Behind Chest Harness is one of the more difficult harnesses to build because of both the assembly, and the endurance and bodily self-awareness of the Bottom. This is also by far the riskiest harness because of the likelihood for nerve damage to occur.

The wraps used in conjunction with the position of the arms creates a larger target for compression damage along the (radial) nerves that run from right above the armpit, down the back of the arm and to the outside of the elbow. There is also the risk of (ulnar) nerves on the outside of the forearm to be damaged. Damage to these nerves can cause wrist drop, which might take months of recovery, if not permanent.

We have included this harness because the body position is representative of many peoples' perceptions of what bondage looks like. Aside from the aesthetic it concentrates a lot of the mass of the Bottom in a way that treats the arms and torso as a single column.

A bondage Bottom should never be made to feel lesser if they are unable to be positioned for this harness. If you as a Bottom cannot be in this position include that in your negotiations.

In addition to positioning, if you are placing this harness on a person who has surgical scarring from any kind of chest surgery, be sure to discuss the best location for the lower sets of wraps on the chest. For some bodies placing the lower wraps below the nipples but above the scars may be reasonable.

Step 1:

Place wrist cuffs approximately three fingers up from the wrist on the forearm. Alternatively place them approximately one cuff width up.

Make sure the buckles of the cuffs are not against the back as they could cause discomfort due to the buckle hardware pressing into their back.

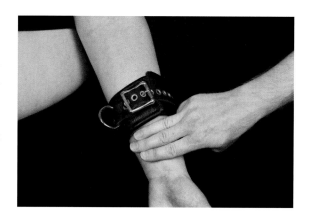

Step 2:

Have the Bottom fold their arms behind themselves in a stacked way with one on top of the other.

Whichever arm is on top is up to the comfort of the Bottom.

Step 3:

Place two single wraps over the top of the pectoral muscles/breasts and attach together in the back with a ring. These can be either individual lengths of chain, or doubled up lengths.

A ring is not necessary for this harness but it reduces clutter with making multiple shackle connections.

Note:

The wraps should go around the arms and sit right below the deltoid muscle (the place where you generally receive a vaccination.)

Step 4:

Place two single wraps over the bottom of the pectoral muscles/breasts. Make sure these wraps are connected in the same fashion as the top wraps and that they lie above the floating rib. The location where they lie on the arms will be a preference that the Bottom will have to indicate.

Step 5:

Attach the lower set of wraps to the upper set of wraps in the front on both sides of the chest in line with the armpit. Use two or more shackles here depending on the length of the Bottom's torso.

Note:

The wraps should sit uniformly across the chest from each other but close together when they reach the arms.

Note:

Be sure to dress the chain on the body while you are making these connections. You may have to manipulate the skin under the chain for comfort. The recommended way to adjust the skin is to lift up the chain with one hand and pull or push the skin away with your fingers in a direction that fixes any discomfort the bottom may be experiencing.

Step 6:

Attach the upper and lower wraps in the back in line vertically with the position of the wrist cuff. Be sure you are not side-loading here and that you leave yourself an opportunity to connect to the lower shackle.

Do not attach the wrist cuff to any remaining slack that might be hanging.

Step 7:

Attach the wrist cuff to the lower shackle with another shackle. Lift the arm up into position to connect it to the lower wrap--don't pull the harness down to connect to the arm. Do not overstress the arm while making this connection. Make the connection longer to reach if necessary.

Step 8:

Repeat **Step 6** and **Step 7** on the other wrist cuff being sure to maintain the in-line vertical connection.

This completes the harness!

Note:

If you find that the lower wrap has the tendency to move upwards over the chest tissue, then you can secure the wrap with these additional steps.

Optional Step 9:

Attach a new shackle adjacent to the lower shackle used in **Step 5** which secures the upper and lower wraps together. Avoid placing this new shackle on the arm side of that group.

Attach a very short length of chain to the new shackle making sure that it is a round-to-round connection.

Optional Step 10:

Pull the short length of chain through the gap between the upper arm and the torso. If the Bottom does not have this gap, then gently sneak it between the skin of the arm and the ribs using your hand to create one.

Note:

Keep this short length of chain as close to the rib cage as possible without pressing tightly against it if you can avoid it.

You want to be sure that it won't compress the inside of the arm and won't be uncomfortable next to the rib cage.

Optional Step 11:

Add a shackle to the lower set of wraps on the back of the Bottom, making another round-to-round connection between the short chain and the shackle.

Again, make sure that this is as comfortable to the bottom as possible.

Optional Step 12:

Repeat **Optional Step 9** through **Optional Step 11** on the other side.

Optional Step 13:

You can pull up on the lower wrap to ensure that it isn't going anywhere.

This completes the harness with the securing modification. Check in with the Bottom to make sure everything is doing okay.

Arms-Front Chest Harness

The Arms-Front Chest Harness is the easier of the two arms-in chest harnesses for the Bottom, but can still be difficult to assemble for the Top. It binds the upper arms similarly in terms of chain continuity (four wraps around, bound to a ring) and also in the Bottom's responsibility to keep their forearms together as closely as they can throughout the assembly.

As the Bottom, the part that requires the most endurance is maintaining the relative closeness of the elbows in position, especially before all of the wraps have been placed. There is a tendency to relax the position after the first wrap has been completed but this hurts the tension of the harness as the second, third, and fourth wraps are attached. Keeping a tight pose will benefit both the structure and the reduction of pressure along the nerves that run down the arms from the wrist to the elbow. If the Bottom relaxes their arms too much then there is risk of injuring those nerves because the amount of tension required to build the harness increases and squeezes the arms in a forced way. Every Bottom will have a different range of motion that may not allow them to close the elbows to a minimum and that will have to be accounted for.

Step 1:

Place wrist cuffs on the Bottom with the buckles facing the outside. If your cuffs have two sets of rings, be sure that they are aligned in a way that one set of rings faces toward the Bottom's chest and the other faces out. If your cuffs have only one ring, make sure the rings are facing away from the Bottom when their arms are folded upwards to their chest.

The cuffs should be snug but not too tight to avoid issues later on.

Step 2:

Attach a shackle to the inner set of rings (if they are present) so that the pin will be facing away from the Bottom and towards the wrists. This avoids having the pin stab inwards and causing discomfort that might shorten the Bottom's endurance and scene time.

Step 3:

Have the Bottom fold their arms up to their chest so that the outer set of rings is exposed to the rest of the harness assembly.

Step 4:

Attach a shackle to the outer rings so the pin is horizontal to the ground. This will temporarily side-load the shackle but as the harness is completed, less force is being applied to this shackle and it becomes a non-issue.

Step 5:

Place a secondary shackle that hangs off of the pin of the shackle that binds the outside of the wrist cuffs together.

This shackle is less about height or position but it is necessary to attach the ring in the correct orientation in the next step.

Step 6:

Attach a ring to the lower shackle. It is okay for it to hang and move in the following steps, but even tension should be applied in order to fix its location symmetrically.

Step 7:

Attach the first wrap so that it lies just below the deltoid muscle on both upper arms. As mentioned, it is crucial for the Bottom to maintain elbow closure from this point onward. Make sure the shackle pins are facing away from the Bottom's forearms.

Step 8:

Place the second wrap in the same way directly below the first wrap. Manage any slack appropriately so it stays out of the way of the harness assembly.

Step 9:

Attach the third wrap below the second wrap in the same fashion.

Step 10:

Place the fourth and final wrap below the third wrap. The orientation of the shackles is only somewhat irrelevant, but make sure all of the pins are facing away from the Bottom. The shackles can all be in the same orientation, or not, as long as there is room for you to work with each one on the ring. As mentioned in Chapter Three, the ideal configuration between a shackle and a ring is to attach them together at the bow of the shackle, but you can be flexible here.

Step 11:

Attach a shackle on the two upper wraps just behind the Bottom's armpit. Make sure the pin is facing outwards and over the top of the two wraps.

Step 12:

Attach a second shackle on the two lower wraps, making sure to loop the bow of the second shackle through the bow of the first shackle, and allowing the pin to rest below those wraps.

Note:

The two shackles should be interlinked as shown with the pins on the outsides of the wraps that they are enclosing.

Step 13:

Repeat **Step 12** on the opposite side in the same position.

Attach a shorter length of chain to the pin of the lower shackle. This length will travel underneath the arms and breasts/pectorals.

Step 14:

Direct the length of chain under the upper arm up against the armpit, beneath the pectoral muscles/breasts, and through to the other side and tension it at the opposite shackle in the same position.

This length does not press on the chest directly--it serves to keep the harness from coming off by traveling up over the shoulders.

Step 15:

This completes the harness!

When you're tensioning the bottom connection from **Step 14**, make sure it is applied evenly and there is equal slack leftover on either side.

This harness could be built from longer segments of chain by performing a reverse tension on the second and fourth wraps, if you so wish.

Body Harnesses / Chain Dresses

With the primary techniques covered, they now can be combined together. Body harnesses can be a great way to try chain for the first time. They give the same heavy weight experience as many of the named harnesses and they also can be self-bound with a little bit of patience.

The goal of a chain dress or body harness is *wearability*. Can the harness be worn at a party or while engaging in other play, or while walking around? These are the equivalent of bondage fashion, and fashion has no limits except one's own creativity.

Designs can be created by repeating a pattern, connecting some of the chest or hip harnesses together, or combining different elements of them to create an overall look.

One example is a honeycomb pattern suggestive of an Argyle diamond motif. It is made by connecting four lengths of chain down the front of the body with shackles. The pattern can be customized with hip harness techniques to make a jumper instead of a dress, or by repeating the pattern around to the back.

Keep in mind when playing with designs that gathering all the slack and tension in the back could lead to discomfort caused by the bondage. Should the Bottom go to lie down or lean back in a chair, they could have all of the connecting hardware dig into their back, which would affect long-term wearability. Because the body harness is already somewhat heavy, having the inability to relax might also pose an issue. It could also be a deliberate condition of wearing the bondage in a negotiated scene.

A tip to avoid this problem is to use short pieces of chain on the back as bridges and make attachments along the sides of the body. Then while leaning back the Bottom will experience only the expected line of chain links rather than a shackle pin in an unfortunate place (possibly next to or on the spine, for example). Alternatively, longer pieces can be attached to rings on the front of the body, travel fully around the back, and attach to the same or another ring. This would have all shackle pins in the front by default eliminating that hazard entirely and giving greater access to the bondage connections in the event of an emergency, or a change of pace or direction of the scene.

Designs can be created from a pattern or a theme and be incorporated into the body harness. Some examples are using the Arms-Free Variant II and placing a triangle ring in the front instead as an attachment point that sits directly over the sternum; or adapting the Gunslinger hip harness to pull down on slack from above the waist instead of pulling down at the (natural) waist or hip wrap.

Like clothing, chain dresses can outline or highlight body features. Emphasis of different parts can enhance a desired projection or perception. Focus can be brought to or away from the breasts, stomach, or thighs.

A triangle ring pointing downwards low on the stomach can mimic the shape of a pubic bone and inspire the eyes to follow where the arrow points. Using a connector or two to bridge a wrap above and below the breasts in the area between them brings focus to the area.

Attach a length of chain between the waist and mid-thigh to enhance a long hip bone.

Consider the directionality of any slack in order to find uses for it later. Attaching a new length onto remaining slack with a quick link can make the connection appear seamless.

Slack can also be intentional. Lengths of chain draped on the body without tension can provide a drastically different look than the same design with even tension throughout.

Intentional placement or reorganization of the harness can de-emphasize areas just as easily. Allow the chain to curve and have some slack around the hips and thighs to prevent it pressing in and creating unflattering contours. Set a connection point or ring near the belly button to hide a larger belly. Create a design that does not go fully between the legs to avoid highlighting the softer inner thighs. With a bit of creativity you can design your own chain fashion to wear yourself, or for a Bottom to wear at the next kinky play party!

Chain tan lines are hard to explain, so use caution when wearing chain bondage while in the Sun.

Chapter 6 - Applied Techniques for Functional Bondage
The Hogtie

The hogtie pose is very reminiscent of the damsel-in-distress trope where a helpless victim is tied down to the railroad tracks with the speeding train coming right for them. It is built from a face-down position with arms restrained behind the back and legs folded at the knee. Being very customizable for a long scene, the hogtie can give a Bottom feelings of being trapped with just enough movement to be allowed a fruitless struggle.

This position has a risk of limited endurance for the person in the pose. In the face-down position the chest is pressed in with the arms pulled back, which pulls on the shoulders and clavicle. Lying on the stomach for long periods of time can cause stomach acid or gastrointestinal issues. Neck pain can develop from being forced to hold the head up or having it turned to one side or the other for a prolonged period of time. It can be made harder by attaching the legs to the chest harness to cause a back and forth pull as the Bottom struggles.

Hogties refer to the pose in general and not necessarily the bondage that puts the Bottom in that pose. There are different ways to accomplish it. The hogtie pose doesn't necessarily have to be a combination of a chest harness and thigh bondage. It can be a freestyle combination of other types of harnesses, such as the mermaid harness. The mermaid harness is an excellent way to keep the legs together and so it follows that the hands and ankles can be attached to it as well.

The limited mobility will vary from execution to execution. In one case, the Bottom may be able to move the legs and hips, and in another they might be only able to move their chest and arms. Different versions of the hogtie can also change the longevity of the scene based upon that restriction. A Bottom that is able to move their chest and arms more easily might last longer in the scene. One that has their arms bound to their chest might have breathing restrictions that can reduce the duration.

The Lotus Position

A common bondage pose is one with the Bottom sitting with arms and legs bound rendering them helpless and dependent on the Top. We refer to this pose as the Lotus Position or Ebi. The Lotus can be a very relaxing position, or alternately, a very strenuous position to hold for long periods of time. It consists of some variation of a Crossed Legs harness and arms bound to that harness or to some additional bondage.

A simple version of this pose might be a Crossed Legs harness on the lower body and wrist cuffs shackling the arms to the thighs. This is more evocative of the yoga Lotus pose and is just as relaxing.

Just like the Hogtie, the Lotus can make a Bottom feel completely restricted and at the mercy of the Top. Something that makes the Lotus pose appealing is its accessibility. A Bottom can be propped on a chair or bolster which reduces back and leg strain. They are not forced to lie on their stomach, which also avoids possible GERD and stomach acid issues. The person putting on the bondage can opt to use a more or less restrictive chest harness - or even no chest harness at all - and still get the desired effect.

Even without a chest harness making some variations to the Crossed Legs harness can provide different outcomes. Placing the waist wrap higher up near the natural waist before attaching the trailing ends to the ankle cuffs can activate core muscles while the Bottom is leaning forward. Placing the waist wrap lower near or on the hip bone provides extra lower back support. As comfy as one can make this pose it does still have a history as a method of slow torture.

Notice we also occasionally use the term Ebi to refer to the general pose. Ebi comes from a technique of binding a prisoner to take away their ability to walk or crawl, as well as restricting their breathing and forcing them to keep certain muscles activated which can be extremely exhausting. With just a few tweaks the Lotus can be taken from relaxing to quite intense.

A more complex and demanding version of a chain Lotus could involve an Arms-Free Chest harness, over-the-shoulder supports, and wrist cuffs shackled to those supports. A short length of chain pulls from the center of the chest harness down to the crossed legs and forces the Bottom's chest forward causing them to activate core muscles for balance.

In this pose the chest harness is already causing compression of the ribs. Being bent forward can increase breathing difficulties. This is a situation to monitor, though it can be the intended outcome.

Putting chain on a Bottom that is wearing shined and lubed latex is the equivalent of expert mode as the lube makes handling the chain more difficult.

Latex and chain pair well for a full-body mummy-type bondage experience with the compression of the rubber plus the restriction of the chain, but there are a few words of wisdom for anyone attempting it. Chain can leave metal residue stains on the rubber. If using a plated metal chain stray burrs could catch and damage the material. And as a post-scene measure, don't forget to wash the lube off the chain after you're done!

Posing for Exposure

As mentioned in the first chapter there are different reasons for wanting to be a chain bondage Top. Some people will pick up this book because the heaviness of chain appeals to them; some will be drawn to the modularity of this bondage medium. Some want to use chain as a means to an end--just a way to hold their Bottom in place for sexual pleasure, torture, degradation, objectification, or a combination of them.

Bondage for sexual exposure and ravishment can include spreading the legs and binding the hands to open up easy access to the genitalia, making the Bottom unable to close their legs or cover themselves. Roving hands or toys can then make the Bottom feel wanton and abased.

Exposure and ravishment doesn't have to be all about the degradation of the Bottom or the sexual power of the Top, either. It can also be empowering to the Bottom, allowing them to feel sexually open and excited. Such a pose might make a Bottom feel desired and vulnerable, or strong and alluring. Perhaps they will even hold their own legs open.

Spreader bars or other non-chain devices such as insertables might be fun to incorporate at this point too. A spreader bar is a classic kinky way to keep a Bottom's hands up and away from their torso, or to force their legs further apart. Include an insertable with a ring attachment shackled to the Bottom's thighs or ankles to make them ultra aware of their own movements.

Variety can be achieved with only a few tweaks. Other ideas to incorporate sex into chain bondage could include the Bottom kneeling or lying face-down having thigh cuffs and a chest harness on; ankle cuffs shackled to wrist cuffs; a rear insertable with a ring connected to the back of a chest harness tensioned to create a bow in the spine, or incorporating other chain elements such as a headcage.

Clothing removal can be an additional objectifying or embarrassing element to play with as a part of an exposure scene. Start with the Bottom wearing loose-fitting clothing, and after the bondage is on, the Top can either pull the material through the harnesses and uncover areas of the body like buried treasure, or consensually cut away the material for an especially debasing or humiliating scene. Make sure to include these elements in your negotiations.

Headcage

Placing bondage on the human head or about the face is an adventurous and risky prospect. Up until now this book has made strong advisories and examples about placing bondage on *particularly fleshy* areas of the body: thighs, chests, waists, and even using cuffs to protect wrists and ankles while providing attachment points at those locations. For a moment we're setting aside those conventions and we're placing chains directly over the top of thinly covered bone: the skull.

There are several things to know that are really important when putting chain bondage over an area that has almost all of your senses.

The first is that you should avoid critical parts of the head that might damage those senses. Avoid putting chain over the bridge of the nose, or having it put pressure on the eyeballs. Don't have chain put pressure on the ear.

We generally advise not having chain running across the mouth. The likelihood of having a dental emergency as a result is very high, and expensive.

Avoid putting a lot of chain pressure on the face where critical structural or functional parts exist. The potential to damage part of the fine muscle control and facial bones is very high.

Examples of areas of concern are the cheekbones, the eye socket (around the eyebrows and next to the outer eye near the temple), and the area below the nose and above the upper lip.

It is possible to put pressure on the neck and spine due to the amount of chain that might end up as a part of the total headcage. This is related to the Bottom having to maintain good posture and balance while the weight on the head is increasing during the scene. There is a risk of having the Bottom lose consciousness because of the strain involved in maintaining posture, or because chain wraps around the neck in a way that causes a blood choke.

Putting pressure on the head can be a tricky affair due to certain risks that are not visually apparent. Pressure in some places can be triggering for people, and they may not find out until it happens. It is possible to cause migraines or other types of headaches through sustained compression of locations, which vary from person to person. Chain bondage headcages require more in-depth negotiation about what could go wrong during the scene.

Some of the earlier discussed risks are applicable as well, especially involving temperature. Cold chain on the head can be extremely unpleasant and could trigger issues related to that exposure. We should note that these risks are not all-encompassing. There are lots of things that can go wrong that you won't discover until it happens.

From the Top's perspective, building a headcage is a delicate operation. Connecting chain segments together requires just enough tension to keep it together, but not enough to damage the Bottom. One of the problems you'll have to contend with is the balancing of the chain in a symmetric way as you're constructing the apparatus. There is a very high risk of the chain slipping off and smashing the Bottom in other parts of the face, or the body.

Good headcages are well-distributed and do not cause chains to shift from one side of the head to other. As a Top it is to your benefit to avoid having hair get stuck in the connectors that you're using. Not only will it be painful for the Bottom, but there is a small possibility of causing a connector to get jammed with hair in the threaded portions. Headcages should not crush the skull, but they might end up being a little tight, as long as they are within tolerable limits.

Light compression in different places around the head, as well as going below or around the chin and neck area, provide opportunities to keep the rest of the bondage from sliding off of the skull. A minor weight shift on an unbalanced and poorly tensioned headcage can slide right off of the Bottom's head, causing an extremely jarring response to the crafted space of building the cage during the scene.

From the Bottom's perspective a headcage can trigger a strong bottom-space reaction that isn't the same experience as with other chain harnesses or bondage. Having weighted material being placed on the head and neck while small movements are happening around you can feel very intimate-- almost invasive. The rattling of chains right by the ears drowns out outside noise. The chain is snug and cool all around the face, pressing just hard enough to not fall off. There is a risk of it slipping a little out of place and causing a pressure point headache on the forehead or temples, or it may fall right off causing a jarring return to reality. Be careful and aware of the Bottom's headspace when removing a headcage.

Freestyle Chain Bondage

All the previous sections of this book have been about making patterns and repeatable bondage, but perhaps you'll find yourself just wanting to create a scene on the fly or add to another BDSM scene quickly.

You might be a kitten and need to attach your tail at the right height. A single column around the waist or the hips is an easy and quick solution. A hip harness where everything connects right below the tailbone is even better. The tail becomes an extension of the kitten player and is very unlikely to shift around or be displaced, even in a pet play mosh pit.

Sometimes the pattern-less freestyling may develop as part of an otherwise organized scene. Pre-planned harnesses are already present but there's just something missing--either some predicament element or pretty addition that needs to be added.

Perhaps you've done a chest to legs predicament but the Bottom still has use of their hands. Using wrist cuffs and a short length of chain, pull the hands up and behind the head like bunny ears and attach to something on the Bottom's back. It is possible that you have a lot of slack coming off of your finished design; take that slack and make something pretty or functional.

There's no hard and fast rule on how much you can add to your scene as long as you have the material, an exit plan, and your Bottom has the endurance. Consider using connectors like quick releases to help get the Bottom into a strenuous predicament to hold. They can be removed when the Bottom taps out, or when the Top decides to change the pose.

It is important to keep in mind how a bondage scene can change when adding elements. In a sitting pose such as this one, adding segments between the Bottom's folded legs to a single wrap around the chest removes the Bottom's ability to sit back. This forces the Bottom into a predicament of engaging their abdominal and core muscles to stay upright. Having their hands restrained behind their head removes some of the control they have over their balance.

In this instance a Bottom could unexpectedly find themselves rolling onto their back and become stuck in that position until they can be pulled back upright. The scene can go from physically demanding to humiliating and potentially painful. It could even cause permanent damage to the head and neck as the Bottom is less able to control their own stability. This kind of pose seems simple but is a bit of a higher risk and that should be taken into account. The Bottom may need much more spotting and attention.

Mummifying a bottom with several individual single columns can be a great way to create a bound feeling in a standing pose.

As mentioned earlier standing in bondage with legs and arms bound can create a fall risk with much higher chances of major injuries. Placing bondage on a Bottom while in this position should be performed with care and attention to their safety at all times during the scene.

Just because we have identified certain harnesses to be designated for certain body places does not mean that they are only for those positions. Try re-purposing the basic design of a chest harness as a hip harness (in the example shown) or a folded leg shape, and vice versa. Play around with binding one arm into a chest harness, but not the other, or using one single column in a place that ordinarily uses two such as in the pose on the previous page.

Symmetry or asymmetry is the preference of the person doing the bondage. Symmetry can sometimes be a challenge to the Top in placing even wraps and using all available slack while still maintaining tension.

Asymmetry can be negotiated ahead of time to be part of the play too, such as doing purposefully unbalanced bondage on the body to provide consensual mental anguish to the person receiving it, or to provide a visual aesthetic and emphasize a Bottom's features.

Purposeful asymmetry is another chance to play with the leftover slack from a "finished" design. Sometimes the leftover slack is already asymmetric by one link. Over-emphasize that by directing the slack in different directions such as on the leg-ladder in this example. On the upper thigh the slack makes a triangle while on the calf it makes a vertical line.

In this example both boots are bound the same way, but the chain leading off from each ankle is different lengths and attaching to different parts of the Bottom's torso and neck.

An inventive Top can create new designs and patterns, such as spurs for a boot-wearing Top before they stomp on their Bottom or a bridle (headcage) and reins for a pony player.

Consider building a chain harness on your human pony with an O-ring in the center of the chest. A waist wrap will provide more places to attach the pony to a cart, and a custom headcage with a bit from your local tack store will provide the *heady* control. You can use longer lengths as reins and let the Bottom experience the full weight of the medium pulling on their head or shoulders like heavy cable.

Pull lightly or tap on the reins to make them sway back and forth for what would likely be an interesting experience compared to rope reins. Be mindful of the weight of the bridle and reins as there are cautions and risks assocated with headcages that were outlined earlier in this chapter.

We've briefly touched on doing bondage on multiple Bottoms at the same time. Organizing people in a chain scene can provide interesting potential bondage experiences for those involved. In complex positions the participants may be strained while supporting each other. It is also an opportunity for them to be intimate with each other in ways they may not have considered before.

Bondage pose involving more than one person. Chain bondage isn't just limited to restraining one person at a time. Pose inspired by Veterinarian on FetLife.

Adding another Bottom to the scene creates many challenges including additional strains on the total material budget, potential reductions on the sustainability of the bondage on each person, and the total length of the scene. Attempting to retain symmetry of the pose can further increase the difficulty. Clever arrangements can be made by linking simple single columns together such as thigh cuffs, and wrists attached to ankles with short lengths. In this way the people are bonded together positionally as well as mechanically. Although the bondage itself is not particularly unique or difficult to execute, *the bondage of the people as a figure* raises the bar.

Glossary

A **Budget** refers to the total amount of hardware you have, sometimes specifically referring to the amount of connectors available. If something is "expensive", it requires a lot of your available hardware.

A **Burr** is an imperfection on the chain that can be sharp and make handling and wearing chain hazardous. It is similar to a metal splinter and is usually the result of poor manufacturing, though burrs can happen because of normal use of the chain.

The **Common Link** refers to the chain link where a direction change occurs and the link is rotated in such a way that establishes intent of direction for the slack.

A **Double Column** is a wrap around two parts of the body that keeps them physically together, but also distinct, usually referencing two arms, two legs, or two thighs. The part that keeps them distinct is a bridge between two parts of the body. This definition is not limited to two of the same body part.

A **Harness** is a combination of chain and connectors on a body that facilitates a function, e.g. a chest harness, or a hip harness.

Plastic deformation occurs when there is a structural change to an object that does not "return" to something resembling the original shape. For example, bending a metal paper clip is an example of plastic deformation.

Reverse Tension is tension applied in the opposite direction from the way the initial wrap was placed on the body.

A **Single Column** (or **column**) is two or more wraps of chain around one part of the body, e.g. an arm, a leg, a waist, a chest, a torso, etc.

A **Wrap** is a single closed loop of chain, that might or might not have slack at the close point. It is a part of a single column.

Credits

We would like to thank the following people for dedicating their time and energy to be models for our book:

LoyalFox (She / Her): 54-57, 112

4thMonth (She / Her): Opposite Ch 1, 71-74, 113, cover

Kenjai (He / Him): 19, 29, 33, 38, 46-47, 59

Willow (He / Him): 120-121, 132, cover

Marti Paige (She / Her): 8, 85-86, 119

Oreo Love (She / Her): 16, 37, 42-43, 45, 102-104

Penny Faedoll (She / Her): 57-58, 91-97

MxHelloKatie / Mx. Spookai / Mx. Spookai Kitty (They / Them / He / Him): 123, 126, 129, cover

Keith Robertson (They / Them): 5-6, 11, 87-90, 131

Ryn Diabolik (They / Them): 5-6, 98-102, 122, 124-125, 131

Bella Luna (She / Her): 80-84, 114

Bree (She / Her): 50-53, 60-62, 66, 75-79, 115

Bootcuff (He / Him): 117, 128, 130

Lancer94 (He / Him): 63-65, 68-69, 118, 127

TonyaHC (She / Her): 2, 105-111

The background photo used for the cover art was taken by Mistress-Sara.

Acknowledgments

Fischer would like to thank the following people who have participated in the evolution of the chain bondage techniques and put forth their own efforts to encourage development and exhibition along the way: Reaper, TheGator, everyone who ever Bottomed for chain bondage @ MDC, Richmond Lifestyle Group, Devab and BondagePupNHeels, The Black Flower, Jackie @ Fallout, and all of those who have Bottomed along the way.

Other people who deserve mention because of their encouragement and motivation to achieve our desires and goals: M_S_B, Sara B, Kali Morgan @ Passional, Lee Harrington, Rebecca Doll, and Katalyste.

Special thanks to Susan Wright for input on the Consent and Negotiations section (Chapter Two), and to Blue Bell-Bhuiyan for sharing input and experiences on bondage for transgender and post-surgical bodies.

Sincere appreciation to everyone who gave feedback at the camp event of summer 2021. Your input was extremely valuable in making this book what it is.

Last but not least, and the most significant is his partner CTW, for without, much of this would not have happened.

CTW would like to add thanks to the person that first got her into rope bondage; RVA Rope for teaching good practices on harness building, body mechanics, and active bottoming; Williamsburg Rope Bite and Fem Rope Hampton Roads for giving the chances to be a presenter and to learn to teach others; and Mister for having infinite amounts of patience while dealing with her inability to sustain anything but the most comfortable of chain harnesses.

About the Authors

Fischer Garrett ('Mister' - He/Him) is a tragically straight-passing, bisexual, polyamorous top. His time spent in the lifestyle has lead him through a journey of self discovery, from once being totally monogamous to being a relationship anarchist; from wanting nothing to do with bondage whatsoever on account of being almost totally incompetent with knots and rope to developing a way to practice bondage in a relatively unperformed and underdocumented fashion. In the past several years he has volunteered for larger kink events as a member of a consent incident response team, a dungeon/playspace monitor, and recently as a presenter for the topic of this very book you are reading, right now! He is a huge fan of costumes and masks, and it is not unusual to know that he is around but often in clever and sometimes strange disguises.

Cecilia T. Winters ('CTW' - She/Her) is your typical queer Millennial. Born at the start of the internet age, she has always benefited from information at her fingertips. She identifies as bisexual and ethically non-monogamous. She has served as a dungeon and playspace monitor, a demo top for a number of local and national kink events, and now as a presenter as well. She enjoys giving first suspension "bondage rides" to people new to being tied; suspending willing victims for long scenes of sadistic play full of laughter, screams, and swears; and suspending herself. Her non-kink interests include reading, watching early 2000s crime dramas, and learning about ancient human cultures.